52690

PR
6045
.053
Z68

Hall, Robert
Anderson, 1911-

The comic style of
P. G. Wodehouse

DATE			

© THE BAKER & TAYLOR CO.

The Comic Style of P. G. Wodehouse

The Comic Style of P. G. Wodehouse

by

Robert A. Hall, Jr. *Anderson 1911–*

Archon Books
1974

© 1974 by Robert A. Hall, Jr.
First published 1974 as an Archon Book,
an imprint of
The Shoe String Press, Inc.,
Hamden, Connecticut 06514

Printed in the United States of America

Library of Congress Cataloging in Publication Data

Hall, Robert Anderson, 1911-
    The comic style.

    Bibliography: p.
    1. Wodehouse, Pelham Grenville, 1881-   Style.
I. Title.
PR6045.053Z68   823'.9'12   73-17163
ISBN 0-208-01409-8

TO ALL MY ALICES

Contents

Preface

This study is intended to provide a first approximation
to an analysis of the style of the leading Anglo-American
humorist of the twentieth century, P. G. Wodehouse.
Several books have been published dealing with his life
and work in general (Usborne 1961, French 1966, Voorhees 1967, Jasen 1973), but only Usborne has devoted
much space to a discussion of the stylistic aspects of
Wodehouse's writing. The amusement that the ordinary
reader gets from reading Wodehouse's light but diverting
fiction will only be enhanced, I believe, by an analytical
discussion of the reasons for our deriving pleasure from
it. The corpus of Wodehouse's writings is so extensive,
like that of Henry James and of Balzac, that only a
sample of his various stylistic devices and of the other
features of his story-telling can be presented in a short
monograph like this. I hope, nevertheless, that I have
been able to identify and exemplify the chief significant
aspects of his style.

Since an objective discussion of stylistic features must
of necessity be based on the analysis of a writer's language, I have not hesitated to draw on the findings of
modern linguistics, at least in their elementary aspects.
Technical details, however, such as phonetic or pho-
nemic transcriptions, have been omitted.

The material in these chapters has been drawn in part
from my previous articles and other discussions of
Wodehouse (in Hall 1963, 1964a, 1969, 1972, 1973), with

considerable rearrangement and expansion, together
with extensive new material.

My thanks are due to Messrs. J Milton Cowan,
R. B. D. French, D. Jasen, P. Lowe, and R. Usborne
for their assistance and criticism in connection with
earlier drafts of this monograph.

Ever since early years, I have had an especial fondness
for the name Alice, amounting virtually to a case of
onomatolatry. I think it was as a result of reading Arnold Bennett's *Buried Alive*, with its heroine "the sweet
enchantress Alice." Less, perhaps, under the influence of
Lewis Carroll's fantasies. In any case, I have known a
number of charming ladies with that name. Wodehouse
has only a few characters named Alice, who are in general tall, statuesque, inclined to be haughty, and not
very matey. All the Alices I have known have, on the
contrary, been most likeable, friendly, cheerful, and re-
markable for both amiability and intelligence. Their
society has been a source of great pleasure to me in connection with music, books, and plays. To all my Alices,
therefore, this book is gratefully dedicated.

The Comic Style of P. G. Wodehouse

1
Introduction

"Great" authors are often thought to be only those who deal with lofty, soul-stirring themes, in an elevated style, teaching mankind the fundamental lessons of human existence. A writer's greatness is, for many critics, directly proportional to his "tragic sense of life." Humor, if it enters at all into the work of a writer who is "great" according to this definition, is only secondary to his main, highly serious purpose. Some authors, such as Vergil, Dante, and Racine, show little or no humor in their works. (Many scenes in Dante's *Inferno* are grotesque, but none manifest enough *bonhomie* to be called humorous.) Others, like Shakespeare or Calderón in their serious work, introduce it only as a foil to their more lofty concerns.

It has, therefore, seemed paradoxical that the professional humorist Pelham Grenville Wodehouse (1881-   ) should have been acclaimed by a number of critics as the greatest master of twentieth-century prose. The dust-jackets of many of his books carry encomiastic observations by such fellow-authors as Hilaire Belloc, John Betjeman, Sinclair Lewis, Compton Mackenzie, J. B. Priestley, G. B. Stern, and Evelyn Waugh, and by such critics as Gerald Bullitt, Eric Gillett, Richard Gordon, and Ronald Knox. We find such opinions as that he "handles words like a great poet," that he is "a superb craftsman," that he is "one of the great verbal comedians of our time," and references to "the infinitely deft tricks of style and the delicious jazzing of quotations" found

3

in his works, and his "capacity for verbal gymnastic second to none in England at the present time."[1]

The few dissenting opinions have been based, for the most part, not on Wodehouse's use of the English language, but on non-linguistic and, to a large extent, non-literary considerations. Sean O'Casey, as is well known, called him "English literature's performing flea,"[2] an epithet which could be either complimentary or the opposite, but which Wodehouse chose to adopt for the title of one of his volumes of autobiography. At the time of the furore over the Berlin broad-casts of 1941, a British journalist (one W. D. Connor, who wrote under the name of "Cassandra") called Wodehouse a "play-boy," obviously confusing the author with his charac-ters.[3] (Bertie Wooster and Lord Emsworth may never have earned their living, but there have probably been very few professional writers who have worked harder and over a longer period of time than Wodehouse. In his defense of Wodehouse, George Orwell called him a "political naif."[4] The quarter century since those days should have brought a better perspective on that episode. Not for nothing (i.e. for something, as Morris Bishop has remarked) has it been pointed out that the effect of Wodehouse's Berlin broad-casts was—no matter what his intentions—to cast ridicule on the Nazis and to serve as some of the best propaganda produced during the war.[5]

Despite general recognition of Wodehouse's merits as a stylist, however, there has been relatively little detailed analysis of the features that have contributed to his almost unparallelled success in humorous writing.[6] We do not, in general, find much more than such remarks as "The embellishment of wit ranges from epigram through exaggerated metaphor to the sheer insistence of colloquial catch-phrases."[7] My purpose here is, there-fore, to discuss those aspects of his use of the English language and its cultural connotations which make the normal reader smile or laugh.

The approach I shall follow is that of M. Riffaterre, involving the recognition of stylistic devices (SD's), each of which functions in a particular stylistic context (SC) against an over-all stylistic back-ground (SB).[8] I have used the reactions of myself and other native speakers of English to identify Wodehouse's SD's, which are then viewed in relation to their SC's and SB's to determine the reasons for their effectiveness. Two preliminary chapters will deal with the classification of Wodehouse's stories and with the comparative morphology of the narratives, which it is necessary to keep in mind in order to understand the basis of his humor. A discussion of his narrative techniques will serve as a transition to the treatment of his language and the use he makes of it, in three chapters devoted to the linguistic characteristics of his prose, his stylistic devices, and the use he makes of variation and pace in narration.

The discussion will be limited to Wodehouse's prose fiction, in general to that of his mature period as a humorous writer (from ca. 1920 onwards). Earlier manifestations of his prose-style will be considered where appropriate. Occasional examples will be drawn from his non-fictional prose (autobiographical books, topical articles or comments). Analysis of his poetry—both his lyrics from musical comedies and the samples scattered throughout his stories[9]—will have to be left for a later occasion.

Notes to Chapter 1

1. The first two quotations are from the dust-jacket of the "Autograph Edition" of his works (London: Barrie); the other three, from Lardner (1948:104), Ryan (1953:737), and Swinnerton (1951:467).
2. In a letter to the English press during the war-time controversy over Wodehouse's Berlin broad-casts, according to Usborne (1961:15).
3. Cf. *Performing Flea*, Chapter entitled "1939-1946".
4. Orwell 1944/45, passim.
5. Voorhees 1966:41.
6. The chief exception is the excellent analysis given by Usborne (1961: 157-163) of Bertie Wooster's "babu burble of clashing clichés and inattentive images" (163).

7. Stevenson 1959:227.

8. For a general exposition of this approach, cf. Riffaterre 1959, 1960.

9. E. g. Charlotte Mulliner's poem "Good Gnus" (in "Unpleasantness at Bludleigh Court").

8 THE COMIC STYLE OF WODEHOUSE

> Those who had got their scholarships at the
> 'Varsity [. . .] used to take their essays to him
> after school and read them to him—an unpopular
> and nerve-destroying practice, akin to suicide.
> —*ibid.*, ch. 19

For the most part, however, the narration is fairly
straight. The dialogues between the various characters
are lively, but not expecially comic.

The last of the specifically school-oriented stories,
Mike (1909), falls into two parts, the first dealing with
Mike Jackson's experiences as a cricketer at Wrykyn,[3]
the second with his activities at a lesser school, Sed-
leigh, to which he is sent after doing too poorly in his
academic work at Wrykyn to be allowed to continue
there.[4] In the second part we meet, for the first time,
the earliest of Wodehouse's saga-heroes, the tall,
monocle-wearing, friendly, solemn, but witty Psmith.[5]
Two later stories, *Psmith in the City* (1910), and *Psmith,
Journalist* (1915), are not school-stories in the narrow
sense of the term, but deal with Psmith's adventures
after leaving school, in a London bank and in New
York City, respectively.[6] Psmith then reappears as the
hero of the romance-farce *Leave It to Psmith* (1923),
after which he vanishes (much to the regret of American readers, for many of whom Psmith was the first
Wodehouse character, and one of the most amusing,
with whom they came in contact.)

Two of Wodehouse's early stories are oriented towards
school-children, but not set in school-locales: *William
Tell Told Again* (1904) and *The Swoop!* (1909).[7] The
first is a parody of retellings of famous stories *ad usum
Delphini*, such as Charles and Mary Lamb's *Tales from
Shakespeare* and their many Victorian imitators. Like
many similar parodies, it keeps to the basic out-line of
the traditional story, but distorts many single elements
for their comic value, and adds minor unauthentic
details to create disparities and incongruities. The gen-

eral SB is that of the slightly artificial, pompous prose of stories retold for children, with occasional archaisms such as *I' faith!*. There are anticipatory flashes of Wodehouse's later farcical style, involving play with language, largely of the rather obvious kind that would appeal to a juvenile audience. At one point, in a speech by Tell, we find a magnificent mixed metaphor:

> "Gentlemen," continued Tell, "the flood-gates of revolution have been opened. From this day they will stalk through the land burning to ashes the slough of oppression which our tyrant Governor has erected in our midst."

Wodehouse's later incongruous enumerations[8] are anticipated in the description of Tell:

> He had the courage of a lion, the sure-footedness of a wild goat, the agility of a squirrel, and a beautiful beard.

Whereas *William Tell Told Again* would appeal primarily to school-boys, *The Swoop!* is clearly aimed at a wider public, of both youngsters and adults. Between 1900 and 1914, several novels dealt with the theme of a fictional German attack: but the immediate target of Wodehouse's humor would seem to have been Guy du Maurier's play *An Englishman's Home* (1909), dealing with the effects of a German invasion on an English family in East Anglia.[9] Emphasis is laid throughout on the contrast between the Englishmen's interest, directed exclusively towards sports and music-halls, and their indifference to the serious aspects of invasion and war. Wodehouse's narration is, as usual, in quite formal standard English, which serves as SB for the quick colloquial dialogue and for the incongruity of informal expressions thrown into the middle of stiff narration or speech, as in the following dialogue

10 THE COMIC STYLE OF WODEHOUSE

between the two Germans, Prince Otto and Captain
von Poppenheim:

> The Prince brooded. Then he spoke, unbosom-
> ing himself more freely than was his wont in con-
> versation with his staff.
> "Between you and me, *Pop*," he cried impul-
> sively, I'm *dashed* sorry we ever started this *dashed*
> silly invading business. We thought ourselves
> *dashed* smart, working in the dark, and giving no
> sign until the great pounce, and all that sort of
> *dashed* nonsense. Seems to me we've simply *dashed*
> well landed ourselves in the *dashed* soup!"
> Captain von Poppenheim saluted in sympathetic
> silence. He and the prince had been old chums at
> college. A life-long friendship existed between
> them. He would have liked to have expressed ad-
> hesion verbally to his superior officer's remarks.
> The words *"I don't think"* trembled on his tongue.
> But the iron discipline of the German army gagged
> him. He saluted and clicked his heels.

Note the intrusion of the inane conversational style of
the stereotyped London young-man-about-town (a la
Bertie Wooster and Bingo Little) into the speech of the
two German officers, especially Prince Otto's use of
dashed twice in each sentence.

Neither *William Tell Told Again* nor *The Swoop!*
is, in itself, a major contribution to either English
literature or the Wodehouse canon. They are worth some
attention, however, as fore-runners of what the young
Wodehouse was to achieve in his later works.

2.2 ROMANCES AND FARCES

The great bulk of Wodehouse's production, beginning with *Love Among the Chickens* (1906) and *Not
George Washington* (1907), falls into a category com-
bining the elements of romance and humor (which, in
his later phase, broadens into farce). Some critics[10]

have attempted to distinguish two categories, romance and farce, placing certain stories in one class and others in the other. This distinction cannot be maintained with any sharpness, since almost all of Wodehouse's romances have humorous elements. This is true even of such early and relatively serious ones as *The Little Nugget* and *The Coming of Bill*,[11] in which we find such typically Wodehousian remarks as

[. . .] Even in the grey of a winter morning a man of thirty, in excellent health, cannot pose to himself as a piece of human junk, especially if he comforts himself with hot coffee.
—*The Little Nugget*, ch. II: 1.i

He was a man with a manner suggestive of a funeral mute suffering from suppressed jaundice.
—*ibid.*, ch. II:4.i

I showed them into the classroom and switched on the light. The air was full of many odours. Disuse seems to bring out the inky-chalky, appley-deal-boardy bouquet of a classroom as the night brings out the scent of flowers. During the term I had never known this classroom smell so exactly like a classroom.
—*ibid.*, ch. II:14.ii

She was incensed with this idiot who had flung himself before her car, not reflecting in her heat that he probably had a pre-natal tendency to this sort of thing inherited from some ancestor who had played "last across" in front of hansom cabs in the streets of London.
—*The Coming of Bill*, ch. I.1

Mr. Penway was good enough to approve of his progress. Being free from any morbid distaste for himself, he attributed that progress to its proper source. As he said once in a moment of expansive candour, he could, given a free hand and something

to drink and smoke while doing it, make an artist
out of two sticks and a lump of coal.

—ibid., ch. II.6

In a woman who had once been a long-haired
dogist there are always possibilities of a relapse
into long-haired dogism, just as in a converted
cannibal there are always possibilities of a return to
gods of wood and stone and the disposition to look
on his fellow-man purely in the light of breakfast-
food.

—ibid., ch. II.15

There are also definitely farcical elements in even the
early stories, such as the episodes, in *Uneasy Money*, of
Nutty Boyd's seeing the monkey Eustace in his room and
mistaking it for the after-effects of his excessive drinking
(ch. 14), and of Elizabeth Boyd jabbing Lord Dawlish
in the leg with her hat-pin on the Long Island Rail
Road (ch. 25).

On the other hand, the romantic element persists,
down to Wodehouse's most recent novel, *Pearls, Girls,
and Monty Bodkin*. The most that can be said is that,
with the passing of the years, it becomes more and more
subordinate to the farcical aspect of his stories,[12] and—
particularly in its more youthful, callow aspect—
viewed from an increasingly humorous point of view.
In his later decades, Wodehouse came to introduce subsidiary love-plots involving middle-aged characters
(e.g. Maudie Stubbs and Sir Gregory Parsloe in *Pigs
Have Wings*, or Barbara Crowe and Sir Raymond
Bastable in *Cocktail Time*), many of whom are among
the most *simpatici* of his personages. From a few short
stories, the love-interest is wholly absent, as in "Bertie
Changes His Mind," "Jeeves and the Old School
Chum," "Lord Emsworth and the Girl Friend," and
"Birth of a Salesman." In a few others, it is only slight
and incidental, and is treated farcically, as in the instances of Clifford Gandle's interrupted proposal of

marriage to Bobbie Wickham ("Mr. Potter Takes a Rest Cure") and the eel-jellier Wilberforce Robinson's sudden rise from behind the sofa in "Uncle Fred Flits By."

In general, it is best to view Wodehouse's mature fiction as concerned with love and other matters seen almost wholly in their humorous aspect, and as classi fiable along a parameter ranging from romance on the one end to pure farce on the other. Conceivably, statistical methods might be used to determine the exact position of each story along this parameter. The development and application of such techniques may, however, be left to those of a more mathematical bent than the present writer.

2.3 WODEHOUSE AND THE "SAGA-HABIT"

If we define a *saga* in broad terms as a series of stories dealing with a recurrent group of characters, there are many novelists, on all levels, who have given us sagas—from Balzac, Trollope, and Galsworthy to Mazo de la Roche—and of course every author who writes a number of detective-stories about a "favorite sleuth" (be he Sherlock Holmes, Nero Wolfe, or Perry Mason) has perpetrated a saga of sorts. Wodehouse, however, has given us, not one, not two, but at least seven extensively interlocking sagas. He himself recognized, relatively early on, what he was letting himself in for when he wrote first one and then another story dealing with Bertie Wooster or with Lord Emsworth. In the preface to *Blandings Castle*, [13] Wodehouse said:

> Except for the tendency to write articles about the Modern Girl and allow his side-whiskers to grow, there is nothing an author today has to guard himself against more carefully than the Saga Habit. The least slackening of vigilance and the thing has gripped him. He writes a story. Another story dealing with the same characters occurs to him, and he

writes that. He feels that just one more won't hurt
him, and he writes that. And before he knows where
he is, he is down with a Saga and no cure in sight.
That is what happened to me with Bertie Wooster
and Jeeves, and it has happened again with Lord
Emsworth and his son Frederick, his butler Beach,
his pig the Empress, and the other residents of
Blandings Castle.

In addition to the two "sagas" mentioned, Wodehouse has given us five others: the tales about Ukridge,
the   Drones-Club-series,   the   Lord-Ickenham-stories
(which overlap, in part, with those about Blandings
Castle), the Mulliner tales, and the early Psmith group.
The golf-stories narrated by The Oldest Member, and
the tales about Bingo Little, also form groups con-
stituting, perhaps, "semi-sagas." Not only characters,
but locales hold some of Wodehouse's stories together
in rather more loosely-knit groups: the London suburb
Valley Fields, an idealization of Wodehouse's boyhood
town Dulwich (both of them in the postal zone S.E.21);
Hollywood; the golf-club; and the boys' schools in
Wodehouse's earliest fiction. Nor does each of Wodehouse's sagas constitute an independent, self-contained
world (as do, say, Edgar Rice Burroughs' Tarzan, Mars,
and Venus stories). The various series are interconnected by very extensive recurrences of characters in two or
more groups. Certain characters, such as the obnoxious
private detective Percy Pilbeam (he of the marcelled hair
and the smut-like dab of moustache), the publisher Lord
Tilbury, or the loony-doctor Sir Roderick Glossop,
wander in and out of several different clusters of personages. The resultant relationships among Wodehouse's saga-casts are quite complex, and are best sum-
marized graphically, as in the accompanying diagram.[14]
This type of graphic representation makes clear
various relationships which would otherwise be realized
only with difficulty. It is evident that the Drones Club—

that association of young men, some of them rich and idle while others work for a living, but almost all of them bonhomous (to use one of Wodehouse's favorite adjectives)—is at the center of most of his constellations of characters. The prime function of the Drones Club is to furnish an inexhaustible supply of young men, each of whom is normally mentioned casually or has a bit-part in one or more stories, until he himself comes to have the juvenile lead opposite an appropriately attractive young heroine. After this, he disappears from the Wodehouse scene, except, perhaps, for a casual mention in some later tale. This happened even to Psmith, the first and in some ways the most amusing of Wodehouse's saga heroes, who was never reintroduced after winning Eve Halliday at the end of *Leave It to Psmith*. The only two Drones Club members to become story-centers in their own right are Bingo Little and Bertie Wooster. Both of them do so by outgrowing their function as juvenile leads (cf. below, § 3.2)

The other characters who are centers of "sagas" correspond to the major-comic roles in musical comedy (cf. below, § 3.3): Lord Emsworth, the amiable, woolly-minded and bone-headed peer; Lord Ickenham, the opposite of Emsworth in energy, bounce, and resourcefulness; and even Mr. Mulliner, the short, stout narrator of tales about his multitudinous relations. Many of these characters are themselves Drones Club members or relatives of members. For instance, Lord Ickenham's nephew Pongo Twistleton belongs to the Drones; so do Ronnie Fish, Hugo Carmody, and other eligible young bachelors whose *innamorate* are sent to Blandings Castle for their ardor to cool off; and Archibald Mulliner, whose imitation of a hen laying an egg wins him the heart of Aurelia Cammarleigh ("The Reverent Wooing of Archibald") is a Drone. Even in the Hollywood novel *Laughing Gas* and in the otherwise unconnected *If I Were You*, the hero of the first (Reggie Havershot) and a minor character in the second (Lord

Bridgnorth) tie these stories in with the Drones by being members thereof.

Wodehouse's many cross-connections are provided chiefly by minor personages. Thus, the American trio of thieves, "Soapy" Molloy and his wife Dolly, and the monkey-like "Chimp" Twist, first appear in *Sam the Sudden* and later reappear in *Money for Nothing, Money in the Bank, Ice in the Bedroom*, and *Pearls, Girls and Monty Bodkin*. Mr. Cornelius, the house-agent and patriotic inhabitant of Valley Fields, appears in *Sam the Sudden*, and later *Big Money* and *Ice in the Bedroom*. Even very minor characters serve this purpose, as do Sir Herbert Bassington of *If I Were You* coming in briefly in *Big Money* to refuse its hero, Berry Conway, admittance to a dance; the butler Keggs of *The Coming of Bill, A Damsel in Distress*, and *Something Fishy*; or the American confidence-man Gordon Carlisle of *Hot Water* and *Cocktail Time*. Of course, since Wodehouse's interconnected novels were written over a span of more than fifty years, the chronological relations that would normally prevail (and which some other writers of "sagas," notably Margery Allingham in her Albert Campion detective-stories and Dornford Yates in his tales about the Pleydells, observe carefully) have to be disregarded. As Wodehouse has said:[15]

> Keggs in *A Damsel in Distress* is supposed to be the same man who appears in *The Butler Did It*, but does it pan out all right? It doesn't if you go by when the books were written. The *Damsel* was published in 1919 and the *Butler* in 1957. But I always ignore real life time. After all, Jeeves—first heard of at the age presumably of about thirty-five in 1916—would now be around eighty-five, counting the real years.

The more reintroduction of characters in a series confers, in itself, no particular merit on an author's work, unless he is able to cast fresh light on them and their relationships when they are seen in new environments. Wodehouse does this by having his main characters develop in the course of time and by making his lesser personages show different facets of their personalities. Bertie Wooster is the prime example of Wodehouse's develop in the course of time and by making his lesser being an amiable but vacuous young popinjay in the short stories about him (written mostly in the 1910's and 1920's), dependent on Jeeves to get him out of scrapes like a *deus ex machina*, he eventually becomes a still blundering but apt pupil of Jeeves with a certain shrewdness of his own. Among the lesser characters, Lord Tilbury, whom we first meet as an upstart publisher in *Bill the Conqueror*, becomes more ridiculous in *Sam the Sudden*, undergoes the indignity of being locked up in the coal-cellar in *Heavy Weather*, and makes an old fool of himself over his young secretary in *Frozen Assets*. The Duke of Dunstable, already a prize example of self-centered obnoxiousness in an old codger when he first appears in *Uncle Fred in the Springtime*, makes himself even more objectionable and ridiculous by trying to cheat Lord Emsworth and Lord Tilbury simultaneously out of the Empress of Blandings in *Service with a Smile*, and is foiled in further skullduggery in *A Pelican at Blandings*. Albert Peasemarch, a pestiferous fool in *The Luck of the Bodkins*, is much more likeable in the secondary love-story of *Cocktail Time*. Sir Roderick Glossop, on the other hand, who is pure dragon in the earlier Bertie Wooster tales, becomes more human in *Thank You, Jeeves*, when both he and Bertie have put on black-face which they then cannot get off. He seems positively jolly in *Jeeves in the Offing*, when he is disguised as the butler Swordfish and is reminded, by Bobbie Wickham's and Bertie's carryings-on, of his own youthful antics, becoming quite *simpatico* in consequence.

Certain instances of non-connection are also evident from our diagram. The most outstanding lack is that of

direct connection between Bertie Wooster and Blandings
Castle. Although Bertie mentions Lord Emsworth and
Freddie Threepwood once or twice (e.g. in the early
short story "Jeeves Takes Charge"), and he is mentioned
casually in references to the Drones Club in one or more
of the Blandings tales, Wodehouse has never taken him
to Blandings. (Such a story would, of course, have to be
told by Bertie in the first person, and would give an
unparalleled opportunity to portray Lord Emsworth and
the other inmates of Blandings as seen through Bertie's
eyes.) A very few of the earlier novels, such as *Not
George Washington* and *The Swoop!*, and some of the
early short stories have never been brought into connection with the others nor have occasional later stories,
e.g. *The Girl on the Boat, Summer Moonshine, Do
Butlers Burgle Banks?*, or *The Girl in Blue.*

It is doubtful whether a feat such as Wodehouse has
performed in interlocking his stories in this unparalleled manner could be duplicated in more serious work.
The effects of the characters' interactions would be too
drastic (one thinks, for instance, of the amenities ex-
changed by the members of the House of Atreus), and
it would not be possible to have them recur except in
greatly changed relationships (as in, say, Wagner's *Ring*
tetralogy[16] or Antonio Fogazzaro's series of novels about
the Maironi family[17]). Wodehouse's type of farce,
however, is just the vehicle for such recurrence, where it
does not involve the reader's emotions deeply and at the
same time allows the author to develop his personages
somewhat more than is possible in, say, a detective-
series. This facility for re-evocation and recombination
of characters has undoubtedly been one of the reasons
for Wodehouse's success.

Notes to Chapter 2

1. For a complete chronological listing of Wodehouse's prose-production
in book-form up to 1969, cf. Jasen 1970.

2. Cf. Wodehouse's own description of his childhood: "My father was as normal as rice pudding, my childhood went like a breeze from start to finish, with everybody I met understanding me perfectly, while as for my schooldays at Dulwich they were just six years of unbroken bliss" (*Over Seventy*, ch. 1); also Usborne 1961:39-41; Voorhees 1966:21-24.

3. Wrykyn also appears in the back-ground of a number of later Wodehouse tales, as the school which various male characters (notably Ukridge) have attended.

4. When *Mike* was re-issued in 1953, it was quite appropriately split into two parts, renamed *Mike at Wrykyn* and *Mike and Psmith*.

5. In the earlier stories, Psmith's first name is Rupert; in *Leave It to Psmith*, it is Ronald Eustace. This is one of the few instances of inconsistency on Wodehouse's part in maintaining continuity from one story to another. (Another is the change of Montague Bodkin's first name to Montrose in *Pearls, Girls and Monty Bodkin*.)

6. *Psmith, Journalist* is a rewrite of the second half of *The Prince and Betty* (American version, 1912), with the Harvard undergraduate Smith transmogrified into Psmith (over in the United States as a visitor) and the love-interest removed. (In this respect, also, *Psmith, Journalist* forms a transition between the school-boy-stories and the later romance-farces.)

7. For a more detailed discussion, cf. Hall, forthcoming-a. In our quotations, the SD's are, where necessary, italicised.

8. Cf. our discussion in § 6.4, below.

9. Cf. the brief discussion in Gillen 1969:107-108.

10. E.g. Voorhees 1966, ch. 4, 5.

11. *The Little Nugget*, although its action takes place for the most part in a school-setting, is not a school-boy-oriented story, since it is told from the point of view of the adults involved, and particularly that of the narrator, Peter Burns.

12. As pointed out by Usborne (1961:118).

13. Reprinted, in slightly varying form, in the prefaces to several later collections of his stories.

14. In this diagram, the names of stories or series of stories are given in rectangular frames; individual characters or groups of people in circular frames; and locales, in lozenges. Connections between stories or characters are shown by lines, unbroken for characters and broken for locales. Where single personages connect stories or series, their names are written along the connecting lines. The names of stories laid in Valley Fields are surrounded by a dot-and-dash line.

Jasen's excellent reference-work (1970) has provided a number of indications of connections through often very minor characters (e.g. Molly McEachern in *Love Among the Chickens* and *A Gentleman of Leisure*).

For the sake of consistency, I have used the British titles of Wodehouse's stories in the diagram and throughout this monograph. The corresponding American titles can easily be found by reference to Jasen's bibliography.

15. Personal letter to R. A. Hall, Jr., dated August 24, 1961.

16. Cf. Hall 1963:143-160.

17. Cf. Hall 1967:68-88.

3

Comparative Morphology of Narratives

3.1 THE INFLUENCE OF MUSICAL COMEDY

In his earlier romantic stories, Wodehouse follows the normal out-line of such tales: BOY MEETS GIRL. BOY HAS ADVENTURES OR DIFFICULTIES WITH GIRL. BOY GETS GIRL. The major emphasis is on the middle section of the out-line, with various developments in the adventures and/or difficulties encountered by one or both of the major characters. Thus, in *Love Among the Chickens*, Jeremy Garnet woos and eventually wins Phyllis Derrick against the background of Ukridge's ill-starred venture in *chicken-farming*. In the earlier version (1906), the chicken-farm is definitely only a back-drop, as it were. It is not until the revision of 1921 that Ukridge, his adoring wife Millie, and their adventures with the chicken-farm displace Garnet and his love-affair as the center of attention.[1] Likewise, in *The Little Nugget*, *Uneasy Money*, *Jill the Reckless*, and the other novels of this period, and in almost all the short stories collected in *The Man with Two Left Feet*, the love-affair occupies the center of the stage. Its development can be relatively gradual, with a certain amount of analysis of the hero's or the heroine's *éducation sentimentale* (e.g. Peter Burns in *The Little Nugget*, Jill Marriner in *Jill the Reckless*). On occasion, a displacement comes about, as when Lord Dawlish transfers his affections from Claire Fenwick to

21

Elizabeth Boyd in *Uneasy Money*, or Jill Marriner
transfers hers from Derek Underhill to Wally Mason
in *Jill the Reckless*.

Beginning with the 1920's, after Wodehouse's extensive involvement with the musical stage (in the writing
of such shows as *Oh, Boy!* [1917], *Oh Lady Lady!* [1917],
Oh My Dear [1919], *Sitting Pretty* [1924], and *Oh,
Kay!* [1926],[2] his plots undergo a change. Their romantic aspect becomes simplified and, as it were, taken
more for granted than in the earlier tales. His heroes
and heroines are more given to falling in love at first
sight; or, if they transfer their affections in the middle
of the story (as does, say, Gussie Fink-Nottle in finally
abandoning Madeline Bassett for Emerald Stoker in
Stiff Upper Lip, Jeeves), it is with relatively little warn-
ing and as the result of a sudden change of mind.
Delayed realisation of the true direction of one's affections also tends to come suddenly, either early on
in the story (e.g. John Carroll in *Money for Nothing*)
or late (e.g. Pat Wyvern in the same novel). Such
changes of mind can be brought about by unexpected
minor catastrophes, as when both Jane and Anne
Benedick realise their love for Jeff Miller and Bill
Hollister, respectively, after Lord Uffenham has laid each
of the young men out with a heavy vase (in *Money in
the Bank* and *Something Fishy*).

The simplification of the romantic plot is usually
accompanied by a correspondingly greater emphasis
on one comic aspect or another of the situation. In
Money for Nothing, Pat's father Colonel Wyvern and
John's uncle Lester Carmody have fallen out because
of a supposedly dangerous explosion that has taken
place before the story opens. Their ridiculous feud
forms the over-all back-ground and furnishes a number
of amusing episodes in the story. Similarly, Lord
Uffenham's having mislaid the family jewels, and his
efforts to remember where he has hidden them, form the
comic back-ground for *Money in the Bank*. As early

as *Something Fresh*, Lord Emsworth's eccentricities make Blandings Castle into a permanent source of laughter-arousing situations, beginning with his scarab-mania in that novel, and developing through his enthusiasm for flowers (*Leave It to Psmith* and most of the Blandings short stories) into his long-lasting infatuation with his prize-winning pig Empress of Blandings from *Summer Lightning* onwards.

The influence of musical comedy and its stylized plotting is evident, furthermore, in the crystallization of Wodehouse's characters into certain easily recognizable stock types, corresponding to those of the musical stage: juvenile leads, major comic characters, and bit-parts.

3.2 JUVENILE LEADS

As pointed out in connection with our diagram (§ 2.3), the Drones Club serves Wodehouse as a virtually inexhaustible source of young masculine lead-characters. Virtually all the heroes of his mature stories, and quite a number of his minor men-characters, are members of the Drones: Ronnie Fish, Monty Bodkin, Hugo Carmody, "Barmy" Fotheringay-Phipps, "Pongo" Twistleton, and many others, as well as Bingo Little and of course Bertie Wooster. Lord Ickenham is not a member, but he is brought there by his nephew Pongo Twistleton, and is welcomed as a kindred spirit by the Eggs, Beans, and Crumpets assembled there.[3] Some of the Drones, like Bertie Wooster, "have the stuff in sackfuls," so that they toil not, neither do they spin. Others, however, have to earn their living. Bertie Wooster mentions (*Thank You, Jeeves*, ch. 3) a fellow-Drone named Freddie Oaker, who writes "tales of pure love for the weeklies under the pen-name of Alicia Seymour." Of the actor Claude Cattermole ("Catsmeat") Potter-Pirbright, Bertie says:[4]

Today he is the fellow managers pick first when they have a Society comedy to present and want someone for "Freddie," the lighthearted friend of the hero, carrying the second love interest. If at such a show you see a willowy figure come bounding on with a tennis racket, shouting "hello, girls," shortly after the kick-off, don't bother to look at the program. That'll be Catsmeat.

Despite the name of the club, therefore, it must not be thought that all its members are idle parasites on the body politic (a mistake which some of Wodehouse's more socially-minded critics have made).[5]

With the exception of the unamiable Alexander ("Oofy")[6] Prosser, who in *Ice in the Bedroom* has found a suitable mate in the domineering Myrtle Shoesmith, the members of the Drones are almost all likeable and bonhomous. To some of them, Wodehouse gives idiosyncratic characteristics. Psmith's solemn but kindly wittiness, first portrayed in *Mike* and its sequels, is further developed in his young manhood as described in *Leave It to Psmith*. Ronnie Fish, in *Summer Lightning* and its sequel *Heavy Weather*, is so insecure concerning his diminutive stature and his pink countenance (which, Gally Threepwood assures us, makes him resemble a minor jockey with scarlatina) that he is wildly jealous of his fiancee Sue Brown (Othello could have taken his correspondence-course). Johnnie Carroll (*Money for Nothing*) is exceptionally timid in declaring his love for Pat Wyvern. Most of the Drones, however, are relatively undifferentiated, and are quite simple in their character-structure and emotional make-up.

Most of the Drones follow a fairly predictable development as they appear in successive Wodehouse tales. In one or more stories, they are minor characters, until they are finally given the major (in some instances, the second) juvenile lead in a particular novel. Two examples will suffice. "Catsmeat" Potter-Pirbright is mentioned in several Bertie Wooster stories, until his wooing and winning of Gertrude Winkworth becomes one of the love-plots of *The Mating Season*. Cyril ("Barmy") Fotheringay-Phipps appears in various short stories, until he assumes the male lead in *Barmy in Wonderland*. After taking the main lover's role in a given novel, each of them disappears from the later stories, except for an occasional mention as a married man who has settled down under his wife's influence— as has "Pongo" Twistleton, for example, after winning Sally Painter in *Uncle Dynamite*, only to be a minor figure in *Cocktail Time*, no longer available as a companion for his Uncle Fred.

The two exceptions to this normal *curriculum vitae* are Richard ("Bingo") Little and Bertram Wilberforce ("Bertie") Wooster. Each of them survives into later stories by avoiding the normal course of development and changing into a major comic character. Bingo Little begins in the 1920's as a personage in several short stories told by Bertie Wooster (e.g. "Jeeves Exerts the Old Cerebellum" and "No Wedding Bells for Bingo" and several other tales in *The Inimitable Jeeves*), and soon becomes the central character in a number of further stories not narrated by Bertie. (Bingo is never the hero of a novel; his predicaments are always minor and would hardly stand being expanded to novel-length.) After several lesser infatuations, he falls in love with and marries a female novelist, Rosie M. Banks, the authoress of numerous "bilge-novels" with titles like *Mervyn Keene, Clubman*; *All for Love*; and *Only a Factory Girl*. From this point on, he becomes the type of the hen-pecked husband, a kind of British equivalent of Dagwood Bumstead of the American comic strips. Bingo's prime concern is to elude his wife's surveillance over his pocket-book and thereby indulge his "sporting instincts" (i.e. his desire to bet on horse-races) or his urge to visit some night-club. By one fluke or another—often through the unintentional

intervention of their infant son Algernon Aubrey—he
is saved from the consequences of the mess he thereby
gets himself into.

Bertie Wooster, likewise, began quite early on (in
"Extricating Young Gussie") as the main character
in a series of short stories.[7] In these, he is rather the
"stage Englishman" of the idle upper classes—long on
amiability and short on brains. His valet Jeeves calls
him "mentally negligible" (in "Bertie Changes His
Mind"), adding later in the same story his opinion
that "in an employer brains are not desirable." Bertie
is dithering, incoherent, and always getting into
scrapes. He is an object of scorn to all his aunts,[8] especially his Aunt Agatha, whom he describes (*Joy in
the Morning*, ch. 1) as "my tough aunt, the one who
eats broken bottles and conducts human sacrifices by the
light of the full moon." He is unable to resist her
domineering personality, and meekly obeys her com-
mands, even when it comes to putting up her young
son Thos in his flat and taking him to Chekhov plays
at the Old Vic. (Bertie gets his own back only once, in
the pair of stories "Aunt Agatha Speaks Her Mind"
and "Pearls Mean Tears", when his Aunt Agatha gets
herself into a jam by falsely accusing a French chamber-
maid of theft.) The only aunt who does not treat Bertie
like a toad beneath the harrow is his Aunt Dahlia
Travers. She is genial and bonhomous, and treats
Bertie well—as long as he does her bidding. (If he re-
fuses to, she threatens him with no longer being invited
to her home to partake of the superlative cooking of her
French chef Anatole, "God's gift to the gastric juices.")
In all except a few of the very earliest short stories,
Bertie's valet or "gentleman's personal gentleman"
Jeeves (cf. below, § 3.3) is his guide and mentor, who
extricates him from his numerous difficulties.

Even in the short stories, Bertie has trouble with good-
looking but brainy young women such as Florence
Craye and her cousin Honoria Glossop, who "set their

caps" at him and want to marry him so as to remould him. They object to his going to the races or to the Drones, and give him such books as "Types of Ethical Theory" to read, in order to educate his mind on such matters as Greek philosophy. In the short stories, marriage to óne of the other of those frightful females is simply one of the various types of disaster that threaten him and that, with Jeeves' help, he manages to avoid.

Beginning with the first Bertie-Jeeves novel (*Thank You, Jeeves*), however, the emphasis changes, and Bertie's efforts to avoid marriage become the main-spring of the plot. Florence Craye appears (in *Joy in the Morning*) as one of the threats to his bachelordom; but there are others as well. In *Right Ho, Jeeves*, the droopy, soupy, sentimental Madeline Bassett misunderstands Bertie's pleas on behalf of his newt-fancier friend Gussie Fink-Nottle, and thinks he is pleading his own cause. From then on, every time that she feels disappointed in her love for some-one else, she tells Bertie she will marry him; his naive code of being a *preux chevalier* forbids him to spurn her love. His bungling efforts to engineer an escape from his self-imposed obligation only get him into deeper trouble, until he is rescued by some stratagem of Jeeves.

This essential situation is repeated in each one of the later Bertie-Jeeves novels, with marriage to either Pauline Stoker (in *Thank You, Jeeves*), Madeline Bassett, or the red-haired hellion Bobbie Wickham (in *Jeeves in the Offing*) as a major threat. His Aunt Dahlia states the matter concisely in the penultimate chapter of *Much Obliged, Jeeves*:

> "How right you were," she said, "when you told me once that you had faith in your star. I've lost count of the number of times you've been definitely headed for the altar with apparently no hope of evading the firing squad, and every time something has happened which enabled you to wriggle out of it. It's uncanny."

Since the ordinary musical-comedy-hero—and, for that matter, the ordinary Englishman in general—regards marriage to the girl of his choice as his ultimate goal in romance, Bertie's efforts to avoid marriage at all costs make him, in the novels about him and Jeeves, into a comic anti-hero.

Bertie develops in other respects, also, as he changes from a short-story-character into the protagonist of a series of novels.[9] Florence Craye and Honoria Glossop do not succeed in remoulding his mind, but Jeeves does, at least to a certain extent, through their constant contact in Bertie's bachelor establishment. Bertie gradually sheds most of his British "stage dude" vocabulary of the 1920's, and comes to use many more learned expressions and quotations which he has picked up from Jeeves. He is still a blunderer, but, as Jeeves says, conversing with Pauline Stoker in *Thank You, Jeeves* (ch. 18):

> "Mr. Wooster is an agreeable young gentleman, but I would describe him as essentially one of Nature's bachelors."
> "Besides being mentally negligible?"
> "Mr. Wooster is capable of acting very shrewdly on occasion, Miss."

Wodehouse's leading girl-characters are, by and large, somewhat more individualized than his male juvenile leads. Significantly, the Junior Lipstick Club, to which some of Wodehouse's heroines belong, does not play a parallel role to that of the Drones, in supplying young feminine leads. Almost all his ingenues have energy and sparkle, often (like Sally Painter in *Uncle Dynamite*, when she pushes the policeman into the pond) taking the initiative when the "hero" wavers in his resolution. Others, like Zenobia ("Nobby") Hopwood in *Joy in the Morning*, or Bobbie Wickham in several short stories and *Jeeves in the Offing*, are feminine hell-raisers, inflicting mayhem on all and sundry, even on the young men with whom they are in love. Bobbie Wickham is probably the most devastating (and, at the same time, the most likeable) of all of them; Stephanie ("Stiffy") Byng runs her a close second. Bertie Wooster characterizes the latter three times in the same novel (*Stiff Upper Lip, Jeeves.* ch. 3, 10):

> [. . .] a girl like Stiffy, who from early childhood has seldom let the sun go down without starting some loony enterprise calculated to bleach the hair of one and all.
> "[. . .] one who is a cross between a ticking bomb and a poltergeist. She lacks that balanced judgment which we like to see in girls. [. . .] She is, in short, about as loony a young shrimp as ever wore a wind-swept hair-do."
> "She's a female upas tree. It's not safe to come near her. Disaster on every side is what she strews."

A few, like Madeline Bassett, are intolerably sentimental, thereby coming near to the category of anti-heroines.

3.3 MAJOR COMIC CHARACTERS

In the typical musical comedy of the 1920's and 1930's, there was always a leading comic role, often tailored to the special talents of one of the outstanding funny men of the time. Leon Errol, for instance, had "rubber legs" and was thereby enabled to stagger and cavort around the stage in a particularly amusing fashion. Joe E. Brown had an extraordinarily wide mouth and a peculiarly mobile face. Three of the Marx Brothers had distinctive abilities—Groucho in making faces and insulting remarks, Chico for speaking with a mock Italian accent and playing the piano in his own inimitable way, and Harpo for remaining mute and playing the harp.

In most of Wodehouse's mature novels, and particularly in those forming part of "sagas," there is a similar major comic part, and sometimes (when, say, Lord Ickenham is brought to Blandings Castle), two. As in musical comedy, the major comic has certain specific recurrent characteristics which his fans come to expect of him. There are, in addition to Bingo Little and Bertie Wooster (discussed in § 3.2), five such characters in Wodehouse's stories.

Ukridge (pronounced, we are told,[11] *Yewk-ridge*) is the earliest of his saga-heroes. As has been pointed out,[12] most of his dealings are shady; he is a thief, a cheat, and a rascal—and yet he is a lovable rascal, with his old over-coat, his spectacles held together with ginger-beer-wire, and his incurable optimism. We are told[13] that he is Wodehouse's favorite among the many characters he has invented.

Lord Emsworth (Clarence Threepwood, ninth Earl of Emsworth and master of Blandings Castle) is, like Bertie Wooster, a cloth-head and a bungler. Whereas Bertie creates trouble for himself by being too active, however, and imagining himself able to compete with Jeeves in brainy schemes, Lord Emsworth's troubles come from being too passive. Amiable, woolly-minded, and easy-going, Emsworth wants only to be left alone to potter around in old clothes and devote all his time to his hobbies, be they scarabs, hollyhocks, or his pig. He is therefore at the mercy of domineering persons like his sisters Constance Keeble (later Constance Schoonmaker), Julia Fish, and Hermione Wedge, and his sometime secretary, Rupert ("The Efficient") Baxter, who inflict all kinds of indignities on him over his feeble protests. Only once in a while ("The Crime Wave at Blandings," "Lord Emsworth and the Girl Friend") does he become so exasperated as to assert himself and override the opposition, giving the sympathetic reader an unexpected glow of satisfaction.

In sharp contrast to the bunglers Bertie, Ukridge, and Lord Emsworth stand the three *dei ex machinis* Jeeves, Galahad Threepwood, and Lord Ickenham. By common consent, Reginald[14] Jeeves is the most outstanding of these, and indeed one of the most memorable characters invented in twentieth-century English language fiction.[15] His head sticks out at the back, and he eats a great deal of fish, which to Bertie's way of thinking makes him so brainy. His favorite reading is Spinoza, or else the great Russian novelists. His range of knowledge is encyclopaedic, so that he can furnish information or give an extempore lecture on almost every subject. As we shall see later in more detail, his speech is an exaggeratedly ultra-formal, ultra-standard English. In the stories, his function is to get Bertie (and often others as well) out of jams, through his analysis of the "psychology of the individual" (one of his favorite expressions) and through the measures he takes, often when Bertie, through his own bungling, is *in extremis.*

Jeeves is an intellectual *deus ex machina,* to rescue Bertie from the scrapes the latter gets into through his presumption unsupported by intellectual strength. Galahad Threepwood, Lord Emsworth's younger brother, is set off against Emsworth primarily by his daring but practical schemes, as opposed to the latter's impractical pottering. "Gally" is to a certain extent a figure of wish-fulfillment. Through the magic of Wodehousian fiction, he has remained exempt from the toll which fast living and over-indulgence in alcohol exact from the normal human frame. In his fifties, he is still a consumer of innumerable cocktails, which have not damaged his ability to concoct clever ways of outwitting his sisters and preserving both Lord Emsworth's absent-mindedness and the romances of the young folk who have been sent to Blandings to separate them from their loved ones.

"A sort of elderly Psmith" is the term which Wodehouse applied[16] to Frederick Altamont Cornwallis
Twistleton, Earl of Ickenham, Pongo Twistleton's
Uncle Fred. As witty as Psmith, he is less solemn and
more lively. He is somewhat of a masculine counter-
part to such female disrupters of human affairs as
Bobbie Wickham. A habitual impostor, he is proud of
his ability to impersonate virtually any-one "except a
dwarf, owing to his height, or Gina Lollobrigida, owing
to her individual shape" (*Cocktail Time*, ch. 10). His
imperturbable nerve, combined with suavity and genius
for improvisation, carries him and his (öften frightened
and reluctant) proteges through apparently insoluble
difficulties to successful out-comes. His reading is as
wide as or even wider than that of Jeeves, but his conversational manner is less pretentious and more varied
to suit his company of the moment. Whereas Jeeves and
Bertie complement each other completely, appearing
together in almost all their stories,[17] and Galahad was
introduced (beginning with *Summer Lightning*) as a
foil to his brother Clarence, Lord Ickenham is more of an
independent character. His appearances are sometimes
against a Blandings Castle back-ground (as in *Uncle
Fred in the Springtime* and *Service with a Smile*), but
occur rather more often in some other setting.

3.4. BIT-PARTS

Wodehouse has invented two-thousand-odd characters[18] in all his stories, and some of them are very
odd. Some, indeed, are mere supernumeraries, given
just a casual mention.[19] Others are minor comic characters in their own right, each with a peculiarity or
eccentricity that gives him individuality. Of these, some
recur in more than one story, or form part of the sup-
porting cast in a particular saga. Thus, the Efficient
Baxter, with his penetrating gaze and his ingrained

(and, it must be said, often justified) suspicion of his fellow-men appears only in Blandings stories. The same is true of Beach, the most butlerine of all Wodehouse's vintage butlers;[20] the succession of pig-tenders placed in charge of the Empress of Blandings' well-being, ranging from the inebriate George Wellbeloved and the odoriferous gargoyle Edwin Potts to the hefty pig-girl Monica Simmons; and George Ovens, the proprietor of the Emsworth Arms, whose home-brewed beer induces a feeling of *bien-être* and geniality in all who drink it; or the Duke of Dunstable, who bestows his unpleasant company wherever he chooses to inflict it, and is tolerated by Lady Constance because he is an old flame of hers.

Some lesser characters wander in and out of several settings. Lord Tilbury, the Napoleonic news-magnate, first appears in *Bill the Conqueror*, as does the obnoxious snooper Percy Pilbeam; both appear later in several Blandings stories and in some non-Blandings ones as well. Sir Roderick Glossop, the loony-doctor (euphemistically termed a "nerve-specialist") forms one of the links between Bertie Wooster and Blandings Castle; another link is Dame Daphne Winkworth, the domineering mother of Huxley Winkworth. Bobbie Wickham, that "lady of misrule," links Bertie Wooster and the Drones with the Mulliner tales. The con-man "Soapy" Molloy, his wife Dolly, and their constant ally-antagonist "Chimp" Twist appear in Valley Fields and in other settings, as do the somewhat parallel criminals Gordon Carlisle and his girl-friend, later wife, Gertrude.

Other, somewhat more independent "bit-parts" are scattered throughout Wodehouse's stories. It would be impossible to enumerate and characterise them all. One only need think of such individualised personages as the gossip-mongering chemist Chas Bywater of Rudge-in-the-Vale (*Money for Nothing*); the lachrymose Phoebe Wisdom and her ne'er-do-well son Cosmo (*Cock-*

tail Time); or the dark, smoldering, languorous but active tennis-player Gloria Salt (*Pigs Have Wings*). Special mention should be given to Wodehouse's unpleasant brats, from the early Ogden ("Oggie") Ford of *The Little Nugget,* through Bertie Wooster's cousin Thos and Bobbie Wickham's cousin Wilfred ("The Passing of Ambrose") to the supercilious Huxley Winkworth of *Galahad at Blandings.*

The two narrators who serve to set certain stories in a frame-work, Mr. Mulliner and the Oldest Member of the golf-club, occupy a position somewhat comparable to that of the emcee or compere of a radio-show. Neither of them is very strongly individualised, except that the narrator of the Mulliner-tales, in the very first of them ("The Truth About George"), says of him:

> He was a short, stout comfortable man of middle age, and the thing that struck me first about him was the extraordinarily childlike candour of his eyes. They were large and round and honest. I would have bought oil stock from him without a tremor.

In this humorous way, a credibility-gap is rendered impossible even for the wildest of the tales Mr. Mulliner tells about the members of his clan.

3.5. LOVE, DEATH, AND VIOLENCE

A great deal has been said in recent years about the role played by love and death in the American novel, with Freudian or pseudo-Freudian psychology playing a large part in the discussion.[21] A "mature" attitude, we are told, has been largely absent from most American novelists' work, because they have been unable to face up to the problems of sexuality and death by according them complete acceptance. Such criticisms imply that no novelist can give a valid picture of life or any part of it, if in treating sex and death (with its accompanying violence) he is at all reticent or limits his treatment of it in any way. Wodehouse's work demonstrates the absurdity of such a thesis, by proving that an interesting, highly amusing, and yet basically valid picture of life can be given without the aid of abnormal emphasis on love, death, or violence. Not that these three topics are absent. On the contrary, they are omnipresent in Wodehouse. What distinguishes them in his work is the way they are treated to make them essential parts of a comic, yet highly intelligent view of human existence.

Normal, legitimate heterosexual love is virtually the only kind found in Wodehouse's stories. Several critics[22] have remarked on the fact that Wodehouse's unmarried lovers never show any awareness of sexual activites beyond those of innocent courtship. True, his young men are thoroughly aware of feminine charms. Bertie Wooster describes, with considerable gusto and evaluative appreciation, the charms of a number of young ladies, e.g. Muriel Singer in "The Artistic Career of Corky," Pauline Stoker in *Thank You, Jeeves*; Madeline Bassett, beginning with *Right Ho, Jeeves*; or Daphne Dolores Morehead in *Jeeves and the Feudal Spirit*. He is by no means insensitive to their physical attractions. Of Florence Craye he says (*Jeeves and the Feudal Spirit*, ch. 3):

> She is tall and willowy and handsome, with a terrific profile and luxuriant platinum blonde hair, and might, as far as looks are concerned, be the star unit of the harem of one of the better-class Sultans.

He describes Daphne Dolores Morehead as a "pipterino," and says of her figure that it is "as full of curves

as a scenic railway." Of Pongo Twistleton, it is said
("Good-Bye to All Cats," and several later stories):

> [. . .] if all the girls Freddie Widgeon has
> loved and lost were placed end to end—not that I
> suppose one could do it—they would reach half-
> way down Piccadilly.[23]

A Wodehousian heroine can be incorrigibly enamoured
of her young man, even if he "seems to possess all the
less engaging qualities of a Borneo head-hunter," as
Lord Ickenham says of Polly Pott's fiancé Ricky Gilpin
(*Uncle Fred in the Springtime*, ch. 6). Yet none of this
implies even the slightest untoward behavior on either
side. As Usborne (1961:141) remarks, "There is no sug-
gestion that either clubman or girl would recognize a
double bed except as so much extra sweat to make an
apple-pie of."

Only rarely does Wodehouse refer directly to sexual
phenomena, and even then the context always makes it
clear that nothing beyond the limits of propriety is
intended. In *Jill the Reckless*, we are told (ch. 4.3),
of Jill's reactions to propinquity to Derek Underhill in
a taxi:

> The touch of his body against hers always gave
> her a thrill, half pleasurable, half exciting.

Of this passage, Usborne (1961:126) has rightly said
"This is as near as Wodehouse has even come in print,
I think, to suggesting that a nice girl can be physically
aroused."

Bertie Wooster is comically alarmed even at the mention of a mediaeval troubadour's love for a married
woman:

> "The Seigneur Geoffrey Rudel, Prince of Blaye-
> en-Saintonge [. . .] fell in love with the wife of
> the Lord of Tripoli."

> I stirred uneasily. I hoped she was going to keep
> it clean.
>
> —*The Code of the Woosters*, ch. 3

In *The Mating Season* (ch. 15), Bertie describes Hilda
Gudgeon as "Madeline Bassett's school friend, the one
whose sex life had recently stubbed its toe"; but *sex
life* is here only a synonym for "love life" in a general
sense. Wodehouse's young men do not normally even
show that they know what is what in such matters, as
in the following dialogue between Pongo and Lord
Ickenham (*Uncle Fred in the Springtime*, ch. 7):

> "I say, how does a chap like that come to be her
> father?"
> "He married her mother. You understand the
> facts of life, don't you?"
> "You mean she's his stepdaughter?"
> "I was too elliptical. What I should have said was
> that he married the woman who subsequently be-
> came her mother."

Abnormal sexuality is wholly absent from Wodehouse's tales. One or two characters, such as the interior decorator Orlo Tarvin in *Money in the Bank* and
Company for Henry, are slightly effeminate, but shown
to be such only by their aesthetic affectations, which
are presented in a purely ridiculous light. Extra-marital
love-affairs are also virtually absent. A search through
the entire corpus has turned up no example of what the
Victorians would have called "a guilty love" playing
any part in the action of a story. There are only a few
mentions of illicit sexual relationships in what are obvious parodies of "bilge-literature" or news-paper
scandal-stories, for instance Freddie Widgeon's "mistaken sense of knightly chivalry" causing him to get
entangled with predatory females and be mistaken for a
"Sugar-Daddy Surprised in Love Nest" ("Fate"). In

Sir Raymond Bastable's novel *Cocktail Time*, we are told, "Sex had crept into it in rather large quantities, for while exposing the modern young man he had not spared the modern young woman" (*Cocktail Time*, ch. 2).

Within these limitations, however, all kinds of love are found in Wodehouse's stories. As French (1966: 68-84) has observed, love is treated with humor, but basically seriously, in Wodehouse's stories from roughly 1910 to the mid-1920's; but then farce comes to predominate, and love is treated much less seriously. The hero comes, more and more, to fall in love at first sight; consequently, from the early stages of the story onwards, his main problem is to persuade the young lady to see the light (cf., for instance Jeff Miller in *Money in the Bank*, Mike Cardinal in *Spring Fever* and his reincarnation Joe Davenport in *The Old Reliable*, Bill Hollister in *Something Fishy*, and many others). Often enough, the young lover is encumbered with a previous, highly unsuitable fiancée, from whom he has to disentangle himself by one means or another. Wodehouse's heroes never jilt their fiancées;[24] they always have to resort to some stratagem to bring the young lady around to "returning them to store," as does Archibald Mulliner when he thinks there is madness in his genetic inheritance and wishes to break his engagement to Aurelia Cammarleigh (in "The Code of the Mulliners").

In their love-affairs, some of Wodehouse's young men and women follow a fairly conventional pattern; others show somewhat more individuality. Psmith is grave and serene in his dealings with Eve Halliday (*Leave It to Psmith*). Ronnie Fish is madly jealous, mercurial in temperament and an easy prey to the green-eyed monster (*Summer Lightning, Heavy Weather*). Johnnie Carroll (*Money for Nothing*) is so timid that it takes a vision of a cave-man ancestor (strangely resembling the cockney Sergeant Flannery, "Chimp" Twist's assistant at Healthward Ho) to encourage him to declare his love

to Pat Wyvern. The timid lover, in Wodehouse as elsewhere, is often a source of humor; his worries and
hesitations keep us amused throughout the story, but he
nearly always gets his girl in the end. (Mervyn Mulliner, in "The Knightly Quest of Mervyn," is one of the
few who do not.)

In the latter stories, written when Wodehouse was in
his seventies and eighties, middle-aged lovers appear,
though normally in subsidiary plots. The first novel in
which a middle-aged couple occurs is probably *The Old
Reliable* (1951), and we find similar pairs in several
later stories. The course of true love does not always
run smoothly for the middle-aged, any more than it does
for the young. The attractive lady editor Barbara Crowe,
in *Cocktail Time*, has to go through considerable
difficulty before she is reunited with her former fiancé,
Sir Raymond ("Beefy") Bastable. Sir Gregory ("Tubby")
Parsloe, in *Pigs Have Wings*, has to get himself rejected by the athletic Gloria Salt before he, too, can be
reunited with his erstwhile love Maudie Stubbs (née
Beach). In the same story, Lord Emsworth nearly "comes
a cropper" by falling temporarily in love with Maudie
while she is at Blandings under the alias of "Mrs.
Bunbury." His feelings for her are so intense that, for
a time, after he has shown her his pig and won her
sympathy for his coming ordeal in having to address the
Shropshire, Herefordshire and South Wales Pig-
Breeders' Association, "by the time they reached the
terrace, their relations were practically those of Tristan
and Isolde" (ch. 5.4).

Marriage, on the other hand, plays a relatively small
rôle in Wodehouse. The only one of his novels to treat
it at all seriously is *The Coming of Bill*, an early (1919)
and quite atypical story of the difficulties of Ruth and
Kirk Bannister, whose marriage is nearly wrecked by the
interference of Ruth's aunt Lora Porter. In general,
marriage is in the back-ground, taken for granted as
the normal goal of both young and middle-aged lovers;

but once they reach it, they have played out their parts and normally do not reappear in later stories. They settle down to married bliss and are no longer available for escapades. If they are particularly conservative, the wives force their husbands to resign from the Drones Club, as we are told (*Jeeves and the Feudal Spirit*, ch. 5) that Valerie Twistleton has done after marrying Horace Pendlebury-Davenport.

When married couples do occur in Wodehouse's mature stories, it is usually as a butt for ridicule. Bingo Little and his bilge-novelist wife Rosie M. Banks are the only married couple to recur in a series of tales, in all of which Bingo is the hen-pecked husband (cf. above, § 3.2). Lord Ickenham and Freddie Threepwood are also hen-pecked, and kept for the most part on a tight leash by their respective American wives—who, however, do not play an important part in the stories themselves. The only unpleasant married couple in Wodehouse are the miserly rich Drones-Club-member Alexander ("Oofy") Prosser and his domineering wife Myrtle (née Shoesmith) in *Ice in the Bedroom*, who compliment each other nicely in their meanness.

Divorce is mentioned but rarely, except in the Hollywood stories, where it is part of the scene which Wodehouse is satirizing. In one of the later novels, *Frozen Assets*, it comes as a slight shock to discover as casual a reference to it as the following dialogue (ch. 6.2), in which Biffen is telling his friend Jerry Shoesmith about his love for Linda Rome:

> "Did I ever tell you she'd been married before? Guy called Charlie Rome on the Stock Exchange. He drank like a fish and was always chasing girls." [. . .]
> "What did she do? Divorce him?"
> "Yes. She stuck it as long as she could, and then called it a day and no doubt felt much better."

Death, as an important element in the development of a plot, is virtually absent from Wodehouse's stories. Occasionally, reference is made to a parent or relative who has died, leaving one of the characters either penniless (as is Psmith at the beginning of *Leave It to Psmith*, as the result of his father's poor financial management), or with a sufficiency of "the needful," as did Bertie Wooster's father. The possibility of death is mentioned quite frequently, however, usually in connection with some more or less comic predicament. Twice in *Frozen Assets* (ch. 4.1, 6.1), Lord Tilbury has all the symptoms of a heart-attack, but recovers and carries on as before. When Bertie's Aunt Dahlia is particularly irritated by Bertie Wooster's fat-headed mismanagment of everyone else's affairs, she tells him (*Right Ho, Jeeves*, ch. 11) to get a rope and a brick, to go to the pond, and

> "to fasten the rope to the brick and tie it around your damned neck and jump into the pond and drown yourself. In a few days I will send and have you fished up and buried, because I shall want to dance on your grave."

A number of other characters also, when angry, express desires to engage in all kinds of sadistic activities against the objects of their wrath. In *The Code of the Woosters* (ch. 7), Roderick Spode threatens to thrash Bertie within an inch of his life, and to break every bone in his body. Nor is it only unpleasant types like Spode that indulge in such fantasies. "Tuppy" Glossop (In *Right Ho, Jeeves*, ch. 15) tells Bertie "In about two seconds, I'm going to kick your spine up through the top of your head." Bertie's Uncle Percy Worplesdon (*Joy in the Morning*, ch. 28) threatens to skin "Boko" Fittleworth, lingeringly and with a blunt knife. Bertie

says of young Edwin, in the same novel (ch. 11),
"There's a boy who makes you feel that what this
country wants is somebody like King Herod." Among
the many other expressions of desire to commit violence
and murder, we may cite such typical examples as:

"Hugo is a meddling, officious idiot, and if I'd
got him here now, I'd wring his neck."
                    —*Money for Nothing*, ch. 4.ii
And this had led Stilton, a man of volcanic
passions, to express a desire to tear me limb from
limb and dance buck-and-wing dances on my re-
mains.
                    —*Jeeves and the Feudal Spirit*, ch. 2
"I wished to pull your head off at the roots and
make you swallow it."
                    —*ibid.*, ch. 17

Much of the humor of passages like these derives, of
course, from the obviously ridiculous physical im-
possibility of the hoped-for events.

When actual death is mentioned, it is for the most part
referred to with one or the other of a rather large number of euphemisms, such as *to hand in one's dinner
pail* or *to stop ticking over*. Of Lord Tilbury's first
wife, Lucy Maynard, Wodehouse says (*Frozen Assets*,
ch. 4.1) that "she had drifted colorlessly out of life."
Of a pair of dead rabbits, a poet says ("Unpleasantness
at Bludleigh Court") that "they have so obviously, so
—shall I say?—blatantly made the Great Change."
The word *kill* occurs fairly frequently in reference to
animals, but rarely referring to humans, so that it is a
slight shock to come across it used casually by Lord
Ickenham, speaking of Barbara Crowe (*Cocktail Time*,
ch. 2), saying "She's the widow of an old friend of mine,
Johnny Crowe, who was killed in the war."

The unpleasant details of death are rarely mentioned:
the only major example that comes to mind immediately
is the case of Jezebel, whose rather sticky end is twice

mentioned with sympathy, as when Galahad Threepwood converses with Tipton Plimsoll (*Full Moon*, ch.
7.iv):

> "Well, what price her playing fast and loose with
> me? cried Tipton. "The two-timing Jezebel!"
> "Don't you mean Delilah?" [. . .] said Gally,
> none too sure himself. "Jezebel was the one who got
> eaten by dogs."
> "What a beastly idea."
> "Not pleasant," agreed Gally. "Must have hurt
> like the dickens."

Nearly the same dialogue occurs between Bertie Wooster
and Jeeves (*Jeeves in the Offing*, ch. 11). In trying to
relieve his friend Gussie Fink-Nottle's anxieties, Bertie
reminds him of the fate of Archimedes (*The Code of the
Woosters*, ch. 5):

> "Courage, Gussie! Think of Archimedes."
> "Why?"
> "He was killed by a common soldier."
> "What of it?"
> "Well, it can't have been pleasant for him, but I
> have no doubt he passed out smiling."

In general, however, the activities of such homicidally
inclined persons as Jael the wife of Heber, or John the
Chaplain (who, we are told in *A Gentleman of Leisure*
[ch. 8], aimed to a nicety a ladleful of molten lead at a
frontier warrior attacking Dreever Castle), are referred to
in humorous contexts and with few disturbing details.
  One thinks of Wodehouse as being, in general, quite
bonhomous, a narrator of pleasant, amusing stories, set
in a peaceful Edwardian or Georgian never-never land.
If, however, we look at the details of the narrative in
virtually any Wodehouse tale, we find a surprising
amount of violence, as part of both the action[25] and
the imagery. There are very few short stories, or chapters

in a novel, by Wodehouse that do not have some reference to violence. Picking out, at random, the relatively
early novel *The Girl on the Boat* (1922), we find only
the first chapter, out of seventeen, that does not have
some violence mentioned as either happening, threat-
ened, or called to mind by a figure of speech.

All kinds of physical mayhem befall a number of
Wodehouse's characters. Baxter falls down a long flight
of stairs at Blandings Castle (*Leave It to Psmith*, ch.
11.2); Lord Chuffnell falls downstairs in *Thank You,
Jeeves* (ch. 9). A number of visitors to Blandings—and,
for that matter, Lord Emsworth himself in *A Pelican at
Blandings* (ch. 7.3)—collide with pianos, tables, and
other pieces of furniture. In *Heavy Weather* (ch. 17),
Lord Tilbury has been caught and overpowered in the
mud near the pig-sty and then incarcerated in the coal-
cellar, so that when he is brought into Lord Emsworth's
presence he is "a mass of alluvial deposits," reminding
Galahad of "one of those Sons of Toil Buried by Tons
of Soil I once saw in a headline." In "The Ordeal of
Osbert Mulliner," the eponymous hero witnesses, from
behind a curtain, a battle of epic proportions between
two burglars, at the end of which they lay each other
out cold.

In his characters' conversation and in his imagery,
Wodehouse makes reference to all kinds of violent
happenings, including many unpleasant forms of death.
One of his favorite comparisons for a man who has been
taken by surprise is with some-one who has been "struck
in the small of the back by the Cornish Express" (e.g.
Joy in the Morning, ch. 15). A few further examples:

   She was feeling like a mother who, in addition to
   having to notify him that there is no candy, has
   been compelled to strike a loved child on the base
   of the skull with a stocking full of sand.
                                —*The Old Reliable*, ch. 6
   I had been dreaming that some bounder was
   driving spikes through my head—not just ordinary

spikes, as used by Jael the wife of Heber, but red-hot ones.

—The Code of the Woosters, ch. 1

He had flushed a dusky red and his collar had suddenly become so tight that he had all the sensa-tions of a man who is being garrotted.

—Money for Nothing, ch. 4.11

The poor old lad distinctly leaped. The cigarette flew out of his hand, his teeth came together with a snap, and he shook visibly. The whole effect being much as if I had spiked him in the trousering with a gimlet or bodkin.

—Thank You, Jeeves, ch. 14

He had heard immediately behind him an odd, stealthy, shuffling sound not unlike that made by a leopard of the jungle when stalking its prey.

—"The Man Who Gave Up Smoking"

A huge hand, grasping like the tentacle of some dreadful marine monster.

—"Something Squishy"

What was going on in T. Paterson's interior resembled in some degree a stormy shareholders' meeting. Nasty questions were being asked. Voices were being raised. At times it seemed as though actual violence had broken out.

—Big Money, ch. 11.1

We must realize, however, that this surprising amount of violence, in plot and imagery, has its miti-gating features. Where actual violence takes place, it has either no consequence in the way of injury, or far less consequences than might normally be expected. This is exactly the situation that prevails in stage-comedy, where trained actors take "pratt-falls" and undergo all kinds of apparent ill treatment, in a way which does not hurt them. In real life, of course, many of the untoward hap-penings in Wodehouse's tales would have much more serious out-comes. On being shot five times, by four persons (George, Lord Emsworth [twice], Lady Con-stance, and Beach), in "The Crime Wave at Blandings,"

Baxter would hardly, in reality, have been in good enough shape to mount his motor-cycle and drive away. His fall down the stairs, in *Leave It to Psmith* (ch. 11.2), would have caused injuries anywhere from one or more broken bones to a fractured pelvis, a fractured skull or a severe concussion. In the same novel (ch. 7.1), Psmith awakens Freddie Threepwood in the train by poising the latter's suit-case on a rack above him, so that it wobbles insecurely, hesitates, and falls chunkily in the exact middle of its owner's waist-coat. In real life, severe internal injuries would have resulted; but Freddie only massages the stricken spot, gurgles wordlessly, and is soon in shape to resume normal conversation.

But why take it all so seriously? In the last analysis, of course, we all have troubles of one kind or another, and we have to die in the end. But this is no reason for insisting upon an exclusively tragic view of life, nor for over-emphasizing the role of sex and death in fiction. Within its limits, and as long as we realize that it is intentionally partial, the comic view is fully as satisfying and perhaps even more so. Wodehouse has demonstrated, more skillfully than any other modern author, how even love, death, and violence can fit into an urbane, cultured, and amusing portrayal of some aspects of our existence. This is one of the ways in which he, like Arnold Bennett's Denry Machin, has devoted himself to "cheering us all up." In the present situation, *ça, c'est déjà quelque chose.*

3.6. STRUCTURE OF NARRATIVES

As Wodehouse settled into his mature manner, in the 1920's and 1930's, the basic out-line of his plots came to be more and more predictable. This was not a disadvantage, as some readers thought at the time. (An old friend of my family's once told us that he had given up reading Wodehouse's novels as they came out serially in the *Saturday Evening Post*, because "you know at the beginning how they are going to come out in the end, anyhow.") On the contrary, it was an advantage, in that the sameness of basic plot gave Wodehouse an opportunity to construct nearly endless variations on the same theme. In this respect, his technique is like that of the *commedia dell'arte*, the improvised Italian comedy of the seventeenth and eighteenth centuries. Of course the reader of Wodehouse and the spectator of the *commedia dell'arte* knows how things will turn out in the end; but that is not what he reads Wodehouse or goes to the *commedia dell'arte* for. His interest is concentrated on how the actors in the *commedia* or Wodehouse will use their ingenuity to introduce ingenious twists and complications into the fore-determined plot; how they will resolve one difficulty but (often) at the expense of introducing one or two others; and with what surprise unravellings at the end.[29] In the case of the Wodehouse stories, there is the added interest of seeing what felicitous use he will make of the language, in description and dialogue; and this is, of course, our main concern here.

To this end, as is well known, Wodehouse was more concerned than many other authors with having his stories, especially the longer ones, carefully worked out in advance.[27] In various places,[28] he tells how he has had great trouble determining the proper balance for the various elements in his tales, and how he has often written a great deal more than was finally used in the definitive version of a story. Single episodes serve as the basis for short stories; more complicated, interwoven sequences, for novels. On occasion, he would start off what seemed good for one type of tale, only to find that it had to be recast as the other.[29] How much importance he attached to structure, and how little to originality, can be seen from the fact that, for several

stories, he borrowed characters and whole plots from
other authors.[30]

In the structure of a number of his stories, the influence of the stage can easily been seen: such novels as
The Coming of Bill and *If I Were You* have a very
obvious three-act structure. In the stories written after
the 1930's, the episodes are somewhat shorter, and there
are more of them, blending into each other more after
the fashion of sequences in a motion-picture. For his
characters, likewise, he has always been very careful to
provide activities for them in several parts of the story,
as one would do for an actor in a play or a movie. In
this respect, also, we can see the beneficial effect which
first his work on musical comedies and other stage-
plays, and later his connection with the movies, has had
on the structure and plotting of his tales.[31]

3.7. RELATION TO OTHER GENRES

That Wodehouse's humor continues and is a direct
development out of the English comic tradition, is well
known.[32] We have already discussed (§ 2.1) his parodies
of "famous stories retold" and of tales of imaginary in-
vasions. A more important butt of his parody are the
popular sentimental writings of such authors as Ouida,
Marie Corelli and Elinor Glyn (in English), "Delly"
(in French), and "Liala" (in Italian). To this kind of
trash, Usborne (1961:20) has given the appropriate name
"bilge-literature." We are told that Wodehouse has
drunk deeply at these "piffling Pierian springs," to
use Usborne's phrase, and that he himself wrote such
things in his younger days. He therefore knew, from the
inside, the techniques and the weaknesses of the genre.[33]
In his later work, he occasionally wrote direct parodies
of "bilge-literature," such as the Mulliner stories
"Honeysuckle Cottage" and "Best Seller." The latter

deals with the love, separation, and eventual reunion of
Egbert Mulliner and the budding female novelist
Evangeline Pembury. The titles of Rosie M. Banks'
works are enough to reveal their content, e.g. *The
Woman Who Braved All* and *Only a Factory Girl*. We
are also told that she has written an article on "How I
Keep the Love of My Husband-Baby." Wodehouse derives some comedy from the difference between the works
of such authoresses and their actual characters—
sentimental but domineering in the case of Rosie M.
Banks, bluff and hearty in that of Leila Yorke (whose
real name is Bessie Binns, in *Ice in the Bedroom*).

The other chief genre, besides musical comedy and
"bilge-literature," to which Wodehouse's work is related,
is the classic English detective-story of the late nineteenth and early twentieth centuries. Here, too, it is
said[34] that Wodehouse himself wrote some, as pot-
boilers, in his early years. In his stories, a number of
direct references are made to such authors as Sir Ar-
thur Conan Doyle, Edgar Wallace (who was a friend of
his), and Agatha Christie. Several of Wodehouse's
characters (e.g. Ashe Marson in *Something Fresh*, Gerald Vail in *Pigs Have Wings*, and Percy Gorringe in
Jeeves and the Feudal Spirit) are writers of detective-
thrillers, and their books are filled with the stock characters and situations of such works, especially the more
hackneyed variety. The Mulliner story "Strychnine in
the Soup" has, as its psychological main-spring, the
avidity with which detective-story-addicts devour every
such tale, whether it be named *Strychnine in the Soup*,
Blood on the Banisters, or *Gore by the Gallon*.
Furthermore, as will be pointed out later (§ 6.4) in more
detail, Wodehouse frequently introduces clichés from
Conan Doyle's and other detective-novelists' writings,
such as might stick in the magpie-like memory of Bertie
Wooster or in the imagination of a child like Lord
Emsworth's grand-son George (in *Service with a Smile*).

Notes to Chapter 3

1. Cf. the extensive analysis of the reworking of *Love Among the Chickens* in Usborne 1961:82-86.

2. Cf. Wodehouse's *Bring on the Girls*, written in collaboration with Guy Bolton, which gives a —probably somewhat embroidered—account of his involvement with musical comedy in the 1910's and 1920's.

Several critics (e.g. Voorhees [1966:38-39, 132-133]; French [1966:48-53]) have recognized that Wodehouse's experience in the theatrical world, especially that of musical comedy, had a marked effect on the orientation of his work. He himself comments on it several times in *Performing Flea* (e.g. letters of Nov. 4, 1923; Oct. 28, 1924; Jan. 23, 1935; May 13, 1936). In the final chapter (14.2) of *Uncle Dynamite*, Lord Ickenham says, of the pairing-off of all the romantic characters, "It reminds one of the final spasm of a musical comedy."

3. These terms are used to refer to various members of the Drones Club, who are classified as Eggs, Beans, Crumpets, and Piefaces. These seem to be simply generic terms developed out of the British habit of young men calling each other "old egg," "old bean," etc.

4. *The Mating Season*, ch. 2. Note that the "second love interest" is just what Catsmeat is given in the novel.

5. E.g. Orwell 1944/46.

6. *Oofy* is a nickname derived from British English *oof* "money".

7. A character named Reggie Pepper in four stories contained in *My Man Jeeves* (1919) was later metamorphosed into Bertie Wooster, when Wodehouse reworked the stories to fit into the Wooster-Jeeves saga.

8. Wodehouse's aunt-phobia has been the subject of considerable critical comment (e.g. by Usborne 1961:31-35; Voorhees 1966:20-21, 108-110; French 1966:5-6). Some critics trace it to the experiences of his early years, when he was passed around from the custody of one aunt to that of another. A simpler explanation may be found in his own remark (D. Jasen, personal communication) "Mothers aren't funny; aunts are."

9. Wodehouse—very clear-minded about this as he has been in general about his own and others' writing—recognised this clearly, and at one point (*Performing Flea*, letter of Nov. 13, 1938) says, a propos of Freddie Rooke (in *Jill the Reckless*): "You're absolutely right about Freddie. Just a stage dude—as Bertie Wooster was when I started writing him. If you look at the early Jeeves stories, you'll find Bertie quite a different character now."

10. Usborne (1961:193) has remarked on the correlation between the names Wodehouse gives his juvenile leads and their personalities:

> Wodehouse had two men and two girls, and he got them all four right. The men were either blah burblers (generally two syllables: Bertie, Freddie, Pongo, Bingo) or breezy buzzers (generally one syllable: Psmith, Jeff, Sam). The girls were either soupy do-gooders (three syllables or more: Honoria, Madeline, Hermione) or boy-shaped, festive little squirts (two syllables or less, and in notable cases with boyish names: Bobbie, Stiffy, Corky, Nobby, Terry. Or Ann, Sue, Eve, Jane).

Cf. also Voorhees 1966:96-97.

11. Cf. Usborne 1961:11; French 1966:30.

51

12. Cf. the discussion in Usborne 1961:89-91; Voorhees 1966:69-70; French 1966:31-36.

13. Jasen 1970:93.

14. We do not learn Jeeves's first name until the very latest novel about him (*Much Obliged, Jeeves*). This curious phenomenon is one more bit of evidence for the often observed fact that Wodehouse's mature stories take place in a world where time has basically stood still ever since ca. 1920, and in which, for instance, Bertie would simply have paid Jeeves in cash each week without ever writing him a cheque or filling out social-security-forms.

15. Cf. the passage from the London *Times* (1959) quoted by Usborne (1961:178), in which Jeeves is referred to without special identification, as Hamlet, Othello, Paolo and Francesca, or Tristan and Isolde might be.

16. *Performing Flea*, letter of Dec. 2, 1935.

17. Except for the anomalous *Ring for Jeeves* (1953), in which the story is told in the third person and Bertie is mentioned only casually. This is one of the instances referred to below (§ 3.6) in which Wodehouse used some-one else's plot, in this instance that of Guy Bolton's play *Come On, Jeeves*, for which Wodehouse had lent Bolton the character of Jeeves (cf. Jasen 1970:211).

18. As can be seen from a rough count of the "Index to Characters" in Jasen 1970:263-282.

19. On occasion, one would like to know a bit more about some of them, e.g. young Algernon Wooster, one of the guests at Blandings in *Something Fresh* (ch. 8.4), and his relationship to Bertram of that ilk. Cf. Jaggard 1967:189.

20. Cf. Wodehouse's description of his experiences with butlers in "Butlers and the Buttled" (*Louder and Funnier*).

21. Especially, of course, Fiedler 1960.

22. E. G. Usborne 1961:25-26, 125-127, 140-141, 174; Voorhees 1966:95, 97; French 1966:75-84.

23. This is a definitely laundered version of a wise-crack current in the 1920's, and often attributed to Dorothy Parker: "If all the girls at a Princeton prom were laid end to end, it would be the Princeton men who would do it."

24. Cf. the explicit statement of this principle in "The Code of the Mulliners," when Mr. Mulliner says "[. . .] the code of the Mulliners is that an engagement cannot be broken off by the male contracting party. When a Mulliner plights his troth, it stays plighted."

25. Usborne (1961/153) remarks on "the high incidence of crime in the Wodehouse farces," and suggests that this may be an echo of the Sherlock Holmes stories.

26. In *Performing Flea* (letter of May 15, 1938), he says "Every time I write a book, I swear I'll never another with a complicated plot"—but how could he have written one with a simple plot? One is reminded of Wagner's original intention to make *Tristan and Isolde* a simple opera, making few demands on the singers, orchestra, and conductor.

27. He refers to his troubles a number of times in *Performing Flea* (letters of Nov. 4, 1923; April 30, 1928; Jan. 8, 1930; Mar. 6, 1932; Feb. 9, 1933; etc.). Cf. also Usborne 1961:16-18; Voorhees 1966:167-169; Wind 1972:86-94.

28. E.g. *Performing Flea* (letter of March 6, 1935), a propos of *The Luck of the Bodkins*.

29. Cf. *Performing Flea* (letter of Dec. 28, 1936).

30. In *Performing Flea*, he often asks Townend for ideas or offers him suggestions for plots. *The Small Bachelor*, *The Old Reliable*, *Barmy in Wonderland*, and several other novels were based on other people's plays.

31. It may seem womewhat paradoxical that none of Wodehouse's original plays were successful on the stage, though many of his translations were— until we realize that prose narration has a very different effect from direct representation in the theatre. There is a curious anticipation of this situation in *Not George Washington* (ch. 25). The main character, James Cloyster, whom Jasen (1970:28) considers to resemble Wodehouse, says of himself "Unable as I was to turn out a good acting play of my own [. . .]."

32. Cf. Voorhees 1966:153-167.

33. Cf. Voorhees 1966:26, 27; Sampson 1941:977-978; Stevenson 1959.

34. E.g. by Voorhees 1966:27.

4

Narrative Technique

4.1. NARRATIVE PROSE AND DIALOGUE

As Wodehouse himself has recognized,[1] the proportion of dialogue to narrative prose in his novels—at
least, in the mature ones—is rather higher than is
customary in most modern novels or short stories. It is
my impression that the amount of dialogue increased,
relative to that of back-ground-narrative, beginning
in the 1920's, after his intensive involvement with the
theatre had begun. A very rough (not computerised!)
count of the proportion of dialogue to narrative prose
in two of his stories bears out this impression. In *The
Gold Bat* (1904), the first six chapters (something over
10,000 words) contain 42 per cent of dialogue and 58
per cent of narrative. In chapter 5, the amount of
narrative and dialogue is practically equal; in chapters
3 and 6, there is more dialogue than narrative; but in
the other three chapters, the balance is very markedly
in the opposite direction. Taking *Uncle Fred in the
Springtime* (1939) as representative of his mature humor,
we find that the proportion is more than reversed. The
first three chapters (also something over 10,000 words)
show 67 per cent of dialogue and only 33 per cent of
narrative; this proportion holds pretty evenly in each of
the three chapters.

The longer narrative passages, in Wodehouse's mature
style, usually serve to set the stage for conversational ex-
changes, which normally take place in quite snappy

dialogue, often in one- to four-word utterances (frequently, but not always, minor clauses). The shorter
narrative passages, intercalated between speeches,. often
serve to describe actions which, on the stage, would be
directly visible to the audience. They permit Wodehouse to be more detailed and explicit (often injecting
elements of humor into his observations) than would be
possible in a play when staged.[2] In other instances,
their purpose is to introduce "asides" by the author to
the reader, commenting on once aspect or another of the
dialogue or the personages. These characteristics are
exemplified in—just to take one example out of many—
the following passage from *Uncle Dynamite* (ch. 2), a
conversation between Lord Ickenham and his nephew
Pongo Twistleton:

> "The ideal wife for you, of course, would have
> been Sally Painter."
> At the mention of this name, as so often happens
> when names from the dead past bob up in conversa-
> tion, Pongo's face became masklike and a thin
> coating of ice seemed to form around him. A more
> sensitive man than Lord Ickenham would have
> sent for his winter woollies.
> "Does Coggs suffer from bunions?" he said
> distantly. "I thought he was walking as if he had
> trouble with his feet."
> "Ever since she came to England," proceeded
> Lord Ickenham, refusing to be lured from the sub-
> ject into realms of speculation, however fascinating,
> "I have always hoped that you and Sally would
> eventually form a merger. And came a day when
> you apprised me that the thing was on. And then,
> dammit," he went on, raising his voice a little in
> his emotion, "came another day when you apprised
> me that it was off. And why, having succeeded in
> getting engaged to a girl like Sally Painter, you
> were mad enough to sever relations, is more than I
> can understand. It was all your fault, I presume?"

Pongo had intended to maintain a frigid silence until the distasteful subject should have blown over, but this unjust charge shook him out of his proud reserve.

"It wasn't anything of the bally kind. Perhaps you will allow me to place the facts before you."

Most of the dialogue, as in the passage just quoted, is of the type that could easily be transferred directly to the stage. This actually took place in the dramatisations of some of Wodehouse's novels, as when *If I Were You* was made (by him and Guy Bolton) into the play *Who's Who*.[3] In other instances, the reverse process took place. From the Hungarian of László (Ladislaus) Fodor, Wodehouse made a three-act comedy, *Good Morning, Bill*; then from this, he wrote the novella *Doctor Sally*. George Kaufman's play *The Butter and Egg Man* furnished the story and most of the dialogue for Wodehouse's *Barmy in Wonderland*.[4] Guy Bolton wrote a play, *Come On, Jeeves*, around the character of Jeeves (having him function as a butler rather than as a valet), and Wodehouse then turned it into the novel *Ring for Jeeves*. In one instance, the process went both ways. Wodehouse wrote the novel *Spring Fever* and then turned it into a play intended for the actor Edward Everett Horton, transferring the setting and characters from England to Hollywood. The play was shelved, but he turned it into another novel, *The Old Reliable*.[5]

The narrative prose, in Wodehouse's mature manner, is by no means wholly objective or impersonal. Even in his school-boy-stories, he occasionally inserted sly bits of humor in the description or narration of events, as when, describing the French lad Raoul de Bertini ("Bertie") and his poor command of English in *The Gold Bat* (ch. 5), he says:

Bertie could not speak much English, and what he did speak was, like Mill's furniture, badly broken.

[. . .] Bertie grinned politely. He always grinned
when he was not quite equal to the intellectual
pressure of the conversation. As a consequence of
which he was generally, like Mrs. Fezziwig, one
vast, substantial smile.

The descriptions given by Wodehouse as author
usually contain humorous elements, inserted into what
would otherwise be purely expository passages. Thus, in
Leave It to Psmith (ch. 10), we find:

She [Aileen Peavey] was alone. It is a sad but in-
disputable fact that in this imperfect world Genius
is too often condemned to walk alone—if the
earthier members of the community see it coming
and have time to duck. Not one of the hords of
visitors who had arrived overnight for the County
Ball had shown any disposition whatever to court
Miss Peavey's society.
One regrets this. Except for that slight bias
towards dishonesty which led her to steal everything
she could lay her hands on that was not nailed
down, Aileen Peavey's was an admirable character;
and, oddly enough, it was the noble side of her
nature to which these coarse-fibred critics objected.
Of Miss Peavey, the purloiner of other people's
goods, they knew nothing; the woman they were
dodging was Miss Peavey, the poetess. And it may be
mentioned that, however much she might unbend
in the presence of a congenial friend like Mr. Edward
Cootes, she was a perfectly genuine poetess. Those
six volumes under her name in the British Museum
catalogue were her own genuine unaided work; and,
though she had been compelled to pay for the production of the first of the series, the other five had
been brought out at her publisher's own risk, and
had even made a little money.

In *Pearls, Girls, and Monty Bodkin,* describing the
appearance of Dolly Molloy, Wodehouse says (ch. 4.2):

Dolly's face was now free of cream. Its absence revealed her as a young woman of stricking beauty, her eyes sparkling, her lips ruddier than the cherry, her whole appearance calculated to make a strong appeal to the discriminating male, thoogh it is doubtful if somebody like the late John Knox would have approved of her much.

Sometimes Wodehouse has sport with his function as historian, pretending to take this role with great serious-ness in connection with a matter suitable for levity. The first four paragraphs of Chapter 5 of *Pigs Have Wings* run:

But what, meanwhile, it will be asked, of George Cyril Wellbeloved, whom we left with his tongue hanging out, his future stretching bleakly before him like some grim Sahara? Why is it, we seem to hear a million indignant voices demanding, that no further mention has been made of that reluctant teetotaller?

The matter is susceptible of a ready explanation. It is one of the chief drawbacks to the lot of the conscientious historian that in pursuance of his duties he is compelled to leave in obscurity many of those to whom he would greatly prefer to give star billing. His task being to present a pano-ramic picture of the actions of a number of pro-tagonists, he is not at liberty to concentrate his attention on any one individual, however much the latter's hard case may touch him personally. When Edward Gibbon, half way through his *Decline and Fall of the Roman Empire*, complained to Doctor Johnson one night in a mood of discouragement that it—meaning the lot of the conscientious historian—shouldn't happen to a dog, it was to this aspect of it that he was referring.

In this macedoine of tragic happenings in and around Blandings Castle, designed to purge the souls of a discriminating public with pity and

terror, it has been necessary to devote so much space to
Jerry Vail, Penny Donaldson, Lord Emworth and
the rest of them that George Cyril Wellbeloved, we
are fully aware, has been neglected almost entirely.
Except for one brief appearance early in the pro-
ceedings, he might as well, for all practical pur-
poses, have been painted on the backdrop.

It is with genuine satisfaction that the minstrel,
tuning his harp, now prepares to sing of this
stricken pig man.

On occasion, Wodehouse will step completely out of
his role as narrator, and will address the reader directly.
This happens several times in *The Girl on the Boat*;
the most amusing of these passages is, perhaps, towards
the beginning of chapter 8.1:

> Nothing is more curious than the myriad ways in
> which reaction from an unfortunate love-affair
> manifests itself in various men. No two males
> behave in the same way under the spur of female
> fickleness. *Archilochum*, for instance, according to
> the Roman writer, *proprio rabies armavit iambo*.
> It is no good pretending out of politeness that you
> know what that means, so I will translate. *Rabies*
> — his grouch — *armavit* — armed — *Archilochum*
> — Archilochus — *iambo* — with the iambic —
> *proprio* — his own invention. In other words, when
> the poet Archilochus was handed his hat by the lady
> of his affections, he consoled himself by going off
> and writing satirical verse about her in a new metre
> which he had thought up immediately after leaving
> the house. That was the way the thing affected him.

Most of Wodehouse's narrative is in the third person.
The chief use he makes of first-person narration is in the
stories told by Bertie Wooster about himself and Jeeves.
We see Jeeves almost wholly through Bertie's eyes; the
only two exceptions are the short story "Bertie Changes

His Mind," narrated by Jeeves, so that we see Bertie
through his eyes; and the novel *Ring for Jeeves*, told
about Jeeves (but not Bertie). The two other major instances of first-person narration are the novels *Love
Among the Chickens* and *Laughing Gas*, told by their
respective heroes, Jeremy Garnet and Lord Havershot.
In each instance, the first-person narrator characterizes
himself through his manner of telling the story: Bertie
as the amiable, vacuous, well-intentioned but bungling
young man-about-town with what Usborne (1961:156)
has called a "magpie mind"; Jeeves as the intellectual
analyst of personalities and relationships, and manipu-
lator of situations; and Garnet and Havershot as run-of-
the-mill young Englishmen.

4.2. LEVELS OF STYLE AND USAGE

Most discussions of usage centre upon what is considered "good" or "bad" in language, with little further distinction. By now, however, linguistic scientists
have come to set up at least a four-way contrast, result-
ing from the intersection of two pairs of oppositions:
that between standard and non-standard usage, and that
between formal and informal style. Along each of these
parameters there can, of course, be intermediate points.
In usage, for instance, one can distinguish several types,
here exemplified by expressions for 'I am not in possession of any':[6]

Literary (formal) standard: I have none.
Colloquial (informal) standard: I haven't (got) any.
Non-standard (lower-class): I hain't got none.
Non-standard (dialectal): A hae nane.

In functional varieties of style, one can distinguish at
least two, formal and informal,[7] and—in most soci-
eties—one or more intermediate semi-formal varieties.
Cultural levels are primarily the standard and the non-
(or sub-) standard. In Western standard languages, the
formal and the literary are (or have been until recently)
the same, as have the informal and the colloquial. Al-

most all non-standard varieties are informal. On occasion, however, speakers of non-standard language attempt to be formal, without having sufficient command of the standard to know what is appropriate. They then use words—especially long learned ones—out of place, committing solecisms and malapropisms, or they confuse their prefixes and suffixes, forming pseudo-learned words,[8] as does the steward Albert Peasemarch, in *The Luck of the Bodkins*, when he discovers highly *copperising* inscriptions on the wall written in *undeliable* pencil. This type of usage has been termed *formal substandard*.

Wodehouse uses all levels of style and usage, with the standard predominating: formal in narration, informal and often markedly colloquial in dialogue. He uses non-standard language relatively infrequently, putting it in the mouths of relatively few characters; and when he does so, it is normally (as we shall see in §§5.1, 2) in a fairly stylized, stereotyped orthographical and grammatical form.

Excessive and unrealistic insistence on adherence to a (usually outmoded and artificial) standard is known as *purism*. Wodehouse occasionally pokes fun at purism, in such passages as these:

> "You have a perfect right to love who you like . . ."
> "Whom, old man," I couldn't help saying. Jeeves has made me rather a purist in these matters.
>   —*Thank You, Jeeves,* ch. 9
> It was Lord Uffenham who broke the silence which followed her departure. [. . .]
> " 'Were,' surely?" he said,
> Jeff shook off that numbed feeling, so apt to come to young men on hearing loved lips utter words like those to which he had just been listening. That odd, dreamlike sensation of having been hit on the base of the skull with half a yard of lead piping slowly left him.
> " 'Were'?"
> "Not 'was.' 'I wouldn't marry Mr. Miller if he were the last man on earth.' Dash it," said Lord

Uffenham, driving home his point, "the thing's a conditional clause." [. . .]
"Postponing the lesson in Syntax for just half a minute," he [Jeff] said, almost gently, "what do I do about this?"

—*Money in the Bank*, ch. 24

In each of these passages, the contrast is between a tense, melodramatic situation and the introduction of petty puristic considerations about "correctness" in language.

4.3. REVISIONS

There are probably very few of Wodehouse's stories which he has not revised, at least to a small extent, when they were republished in book-form after appearing in magazines, or when they came out as reprints in new editions. The extent of the revisions differs markedly from one tale to another: in some instances it is slight, in others moderate, and in still others it is quite extensive. In some, the story itself was altered, either by introducing a different series of events or by changes in emphasis. In others, material was either added or subtracted, but without a major change in the story.

The least important changes are those involving mere orthographical adaptations, as between minor points of British and American spelling. Words like *humour*, *favour*, etc. of course have -*our* in the British versions, but -*or* in the American editions, and similarly for British *cheque* versus American *check* and the like. The British editions are in general freer with the use of hyphens than are the American, due to the increasing phobia which American editors and printers have developed vis-a-vis the hyphen over the last half-century or more.[9] In vocabulary, also, one occasionally finds the British term substituted for the American or vice versa—probably by some copy-editor in the publisher's office. Once in a while, a slip-up occurs. In "Jeeves and the Old School Chum," for instance, British *petrol* was duly replaced by *gas(oline)* in the American edition, but *dickey* was left in ("Bingo and Mrs. Bingo in their car, and the Pyke in mine, with Jeeves sitting behind in the dickey"). Some-one in the editorial office obviously did not know that this word referred to what, in American roadsters of the time, was called a *rumble-seat*.

The ending of *Leave It to Psmith* constitutes a good example of a simple change in plot, achieved merely by substituting one set of occurrences for another. After the original version had appeared serially in the *Saturday Evening Post* (in February and March of 1923), Wodehouse wrote to Townend[10] "I have had a stream of letters cursing the end of *Leave It to Psmith*, and I shall have to rewrite it." This was not, as some literary critics have assumed,[11] due to some structural short-coming. It was simply because, in Chapter 13.4, Wode-house originally had the "villain" and "villainess," Edward Cootes and Aileen Peavey, corner Psmith and Eve Halliday take away Lady Constance Keeble's neck-lace at gun-point. In the revised version, a sudden dis-turbance enables Psmith to disarm Cootes and regain the upper hand. The out-come of the story is the same, but in the new version Psmith and Eve retain possession of the jewels and use them to obtain money directly from Mr. Keeble according to their original plan.

Comparing these two resolutions of the plot, one can see that no basic structural difficulty was involved. The earlier version was slightly more realistic; the second, as observed by Voorhees,[12] less realistic and more in line with Wodehouse's later farcical manner. I remember feeling slightly disappointed when, as a twelve-year-old in 1923, I read *Leave It to Psmith* in the *Post*, and Wode-house had the "villain" and "villainess"[13] be successful and get away with the swag. Clearly, what displeased his complaining readers was the discomfiture of the hero and heroine. From this point on, Wodehouse always had his hero and heroine prove successful in the end, even at the price of unrealistic and even farcical chance events.[14] Readers of light fiction do not like to have their fantasy-worlds impinged upon by even slightly realistic events which interfere with a wholly "happy" dénouement.

A considerably more extensive rewrite-job was involved when Wodehouse did the entire first half of *The Luck of the Bodkins* over, creating a sizeable difference between the first (English) version and that which finally appeared in the United States.[15] The basic plot remained the same: Monty Bodkin has, in his effort to keep the love of his fiancee Gertrude Butterwick, all kinds of complications in the course of a trans-Atlantic voyage, which ensue as a result of his getting entangled with the efforts of the movie-magnate Ivor Llewellyn to smuggle a diamond necklace into the United States. In addition to cutting out a fair amount of both dialogue and narrator's obiter dicta, Wodehouse telescoped several episodes and rearranged others. In both versions, the first scene of the story is set in Cannes, but it is considerably shortened in the American version. In the earlier version, the next part of the story was presented in two separate scenes, one on a boat-train leaving Waterloo Station for Southampton, and the other on board the ship after its departure from that port. The later version starts the scene on the docks at Southampton, just before the ship's departure. Much of the dialogue is cut, and some of it is transferred to later scenes. However, the speeches of the chief comic character, the self-important, malapropistic, pestiferaceous steward Albert Peasemarch, are left pretty much intact.

In other instances, Wodehouse accomplished his changes primarily through cutting. In this way, the 1921 version of *Love Among the Chickens* omits a good deal of the material connected with Jeremy Garnet's and Phyllis Derrick's love-affair, shifting the emphasis away from them to the more comical aspect of the story, the trials and tribulations of Ukridge and his wife Millie in trying to run a chicken-farm.[16] A similar, though much less drastic, process of cutting took place in the revision of *Uncle Fred in the Springtime*. In this case, he made a few cuts in chapter 3, and fairly extensive ones in chapter 10, removing passages of dialogue which did not contribute to furthering the action. Yet it cannot be said that these revisions were altogether beneficial. The American version of *The Luck of the Bodkins* seems, in comparision with the English version, excessively compact and tense, lacking the relaxed atmosphere and some of the Wodehousian geniality which one normally expects.[17] In *Uncle Fred in the Springtime*, the excised passages illustrate Lord Ickenham's command of banter, his character as a "buzzer," and one misses, in the American version, such Ickenhamian persiflage as the following (ch. 3):

> "What did you think of Mustard?"
> "He seemed all right."
> "He's a splended fellow. Saved my life once, when he was my batman in the war. It was outside Festubert, and there was a lot of heavy shelling going on, and we had sat down to lunch, and I was just about to dig into the tinned salmon, when Mustard whispered in my ear 'I wouldn't,' and I didn't."

When Wodehouse cut drastically the dialogue between Lord Ickenham, who is pretending to be the loony-doctor Sir Roderick Glossop, and Horace Davenport in chapter 10, the reader lost such laughter-arousing give-and-take as:

> "Tell me, do we feel a little heavy in the head at times?"
> "We do, rather."
> "Do we see floating spots?"
> "We do, a few."
> "But we do not hear voices and think we are being followed about by little men with beards?"

"No."
"Then all is well. We have just gone off the rails a little, that is all. We must relax. We must take care of ourself. We must avoid rich foods and not go to too many Marx Brothers pictures."

In general, Wodehouse's revisions have been beneficial to his stories. What Usborne says (1961:160) of the "Bertie Wodehouse" style is true of Wodehouse's writing as a whole:

> The best parodies of Bertie's style are by Wodehouse himself when he lets a page go to the printer without quite the necessary polish. Then you are probably reading the sixth draft, rather than the tenth.

In a few instances, however, such as those we have just discussed, we will nevertheless go to the earlier, more relaxed and genial and hence more amusing version to get the true bonhomous Wodehouse.

Notes to Chapter 4

1. *Performing Flea*, letter of June 30, 1945.
2. Such play-wrights as Shaw and Barrie, writing as much for readers as for performance in the theatre, have done the same kind of thing, introducing a great deal of description (some would say palaver) into their stage-directions. Cf. also the observations of Usborne 1961:160-161.
3. The three-act structure of *If I Were You* is very obvious, with the first and third acts (ch. 1-10 and 21-25) set in the drawing-room of the country-house at Langley End, and the second (ch. 11-20) in Price's barber-shop in the Brompton Road.
4. Cf. Usborne 1961:120.
5. Cf. Usborne 1961:119-120 for discussion of these instances.
6. These examples have been adapted from Bloomfield 1933:52.
7. Cf. Kenyon 1948.
8. Discussed by Bloomfield (1933:153) with the examples *scrumptious, rambunctious,* and *absquatulate* ('leave in a hurry').
9. For the entire *vexata quaestio* of hyphenation, cf. Hall 1964c.
10. *Performing Flea*, letter of May 2, 1923.
11. E.G. Usborne 1961:76-77: "Wodehouse says that he had had trouble with the last half of *Leave It to Psmith*, and, indeed, had to rewrite it after

the first edition." In actuality, the only major revision (as I have observed by checking the book directly against the version in the magazine) affected the episode discussed here. For a more detailed discussion, cf. Hall, forthcoming-b.

12. "Even Psmith, who, of all of Wodehouse's heroes, comes closest to playing the role of Raffles, overcomes a gunman with farcical assistance. Bound and gagged [no, merely terrorized—RAHjr] in a second-floor room of a cottage, Freddie Threepwood thrashes around and sticks his foot through the flimsy ceiling, thus providing the assistance that Psmith needs" (Voorhees 1966:98).

13. Not that Wodehouse's "baddies" are really villainous. As French (1966:70) observes, "Since crime occurs frequently, though always as a comic complication, there are criminals [. . .]. Wodehouse loves them almost as much as he loves Ukridge. Like him, they are always foiled, and always, in spite of their deplorable activities, essentially innocent."

14. For instance, a similar situation in *Big Money* (1931) is resolved when Lord Biskerton chops a hole through the flimsy party-wall that separates two houses. In later stories, the crooks sometimes get an apparent victory, which turns out to be a hollow one: thus, "Soapy" and Dolly Molloy get away with an empty jar (which they think contains the jewels) at the end of *Money in the Bank*, and "Chimp" Twist does likewise with a string of fake pearls at the end of *Pearls, Girls, and Monty Bodkin*.

15. For the first time in over two decades, Wodehouse had a story rejected by the *Saturday Evening Post* when they turned down *The Luck of the Bodkins* in 1935 (cf. *Performing Flea*, letter of Feb. 4, 1935). He then redid it, as he wrote Townend (letter of Mar. 6, 1935): "I got 25,000 words out of *The Luck of the Bodkins* without any trouble at all, but not by paring down scenes. I reconstructed the first half of the story entirely, taking advantage of a really sound criticism from Reeves Shaw to eliminate one situation entirely. Isn't it odd how one can spoil a story by being too leisurely in telling it?"

16. Cf. Usborne 1961:82-83.

17. On first reading the English version, which I came to know only some years after reading the American edition, I sensed the (to my notion) marked superiority of the former, and took it to be the later, improved version. It was only from Jasen (1970:160-161) that I learned that the converse was true.

5

Linguistic Characteristics

In this chapter, I shall discuss briefly the structural
and lexical features to be found in Wodehouse's prose,
without reference to the use that he makes of them.[1]
This latter topic will be taken up in the following two
chapters.

5.1. ORTHOGRAPHY AND PHONOLOGY

Occasionally, authors may be aware, even acutely
aware, of differences in speech, as was Mark Twain [2]
and may do their best to represent those differences in
the way they transcribe their characters' talk. The reading public, however, is so conditioned to reject all
material that is not presented in purely traditional
spelling that virtually no writer ever introduces any more
accurate type of transcription (e.g. the alphabet of the
International Phonetic Association). Wodehouse is no
exception to this principle. We find him using only the
conventional orthography of the languages he introduces—English, of course, with occasional phrases
or sentences in French and Latin, with a little German.
As mentioned in the previous chapter (§ 4.3), the slight
differences in spelling between British and American
practice have normally been adjusted automatically
by copy-editors or printers.

67

Wodehouse himself is, naturally, a native speaker of British English. Those who have heard him speak on radio or television say that his accent is that of a normal speaker of "received standard." In all except a few instances, it is tacitly assumed in his stories that, among speakers of standard English, differences in pronunciation are negligible.[3] Psmith passes himself off as a Canadian when he goes to Blandings, with no-one commenting on the difference. Once in a while, an Americanism in a character's pronunciation may be made the basis for a humorous passage, as when, in *Big Money* (ch. 5), Kitchie Valentine "made an observation which was neither 'Yep,' 'Yop,' nor 'Yup,' but a musical blend of all three." "Tubby" Vanringham and his fiancee Prudence Whittaker, in *Summer Moonshine*, quarrel over his American pronunciation. The lah-de-dah Kensington-trained secretary says to Tubby in Chapter I:

> "I would no more dream of saying 'ouseboat' when I would of employing a vulgarism like 'Yup' when I meant 'Yes,' or saying 'mustash' when I meant 'moustarsh,' or 'tomayto' when I meant 'tomarto,' or—" [. . .]
> "I suppose," said Tubby [. . .] "that when you go out to lunch with that boy friend who sends you jewellery, you say 'Oh, Percy, will you please pass the potartoes?'"

Prudence's objections to Tubby's American accent are made more comic by her own use of the affected, formal sub-standard phonology of some upwardly mobile British lower-middle-class women, who make automatic substitutions of sounds in positions where they do not belong, as in what Wodehouse and others spell *quate* for 'quite' and *moddom* for 'madam'. She and others (e.g. the intellectually inclined secretary Lavender Briggs in *Service with a Smile*, and the pompous-ass politician Clifford Gandle in "Mr. Potter Takes a Rest Cure") exaggerate the neutral vowel which has replaced *r* at the end of such words as *desire, here, there* in south-east British English. They make a separate syllable of it, which Wodehouse represents with the spellings *desi-ah, hee-yah,* and *they-ah* respectively. Gandle's pronunciation of the final vowel in such words as *Nature* or *razor,* exaggerated and lowered toward a sound like Italian *a,* is spelled *Na-chah, ra-zah.* Much the same phenomenon is represented by *aw* in Percy Gorringe's referring to his mother as *Moth-aw (Jeeves and the Feudal Spirit).*

Where Wodehouse introduces sub-standard speech into his dialogues, he does so, in general, with the more or less conventional orthographic devices which are common property. British lower-class speech is characterized especially by the pronunciation of words like *gone* or *small* with the same vowel as its speakers have in *torn, short.* Wodehouse represents this, rightly, with *or,* as when Hash Todhunter (the ship's cook in *Sam the Sudden*) speaks of some-one as having *gorn,* or, in the same story (ch. 5), a group of men in a bar argue over whether the Duke of York has a "smorl clipped moustache." The lower-class habit of making an affirmative assertion with a syllabic (retroflex) *r* is represented, e.g. in "Archibald and the Masses" and "The Ordeal of Osbert Mulliner," by "R." The lower-class Londoner's exclamation of surprise is *Coo!*, and the upper-class variation thereof is *Cor!*, as in the speech of the parvenu publishing-tycoon Lord Tilbury. Specifically Cockney features include the use of the vowel of *mite* in words like *mate,* as in the London girl Gladys' pronunciation of *playing* (spelled *pliying*) in "Lord Emsworth and the Girl Friend"; the merger of the vowel of *hem* with that of *ham,* as in her reference to *jem sengwidges* 'jam sandwiches' (which Lord Emsworth finds himself starting to imitate); and the monosyllabic variant *flarze* for 'flowers'. Cockneys notoriously lose initial *h,* with resultant linking between word-final consonants and the initial vowels of words whose aitch has been dropped,

as when, in "The Passing of Ambrose," a commission-
aire says to Algernon Crufts:

> "Here's your rat. A little the worse for wear, this
> sat is, I'm afraid, sir. A gentleman happened to step
> on it. You can't step on a nat, not without hurting
> it. That tat is not the yat it was."

American lower-class speech is represented in a decidedly stylized way, also. Beginning with the second
half of *The Prince and Betty* (later transmogrified into
Psmith, Journalist), and continuing through *A Gentleman of Leisure* and *The Small Bachelor*) several of
Wodehouse's gangsters, prize-fighters, and similar New
York types regularly substitute *oi* for *ur* in words like
moider 'murder', and *t* or *d* for *th* in *wit'* 'with', *de* 'the',
and so on. His American crooks, especially Dolly Mol-
loy, are given to saying *yay-ess* for 'yes'. These are
nothing more than the common nineteenth- and early
twentieth-century stereotype of the way such people
were supposed to talk, and are even less realistic than
Wodehouse's representation of lower-class English
speech.[1]

For sounds or phonological features that do not
normally find representation in English spelling, Wodehouse (like virtually all others) has recourse to the closest
analogy in conventional orthography. The unstressed
vowel which occurs between consonants, when a word
is stretched out into more syllables than usual, sounds
to British ears like the unstressed variant of their *er*.
Hence, when (in "The Crime Wave at Blandings") Lord
Bosham's son George is confronted with the necessity of
having a tutor during the summer holidays, he ex-
claims loudly "Tew-tor? Ter-YEW-tor?". Wodehouse
also uses *er* to represent various aberrant stressed vowel-
sounds, as in Lord Uffenham's *yerss* for 'yes', and also
bersicle for 'bicycle' and *verlent* for 'violent' (*The Code
of the Woosters*, ch. 4). An anonymous member of the
proletariat, girding at Lord Hoddesdon in *Big Money*
(ch. 6.2), says to him:

"Do you know what would happen to you in Moscow? Somebody—as it might be Stayling—would come along and 'e'd look at that 'at and 'e'd say, 'What are you doing, you Burjoice, swanking 'round in a 'at like that?' "

with the spellings *Stayling* for 'Stalin' and *burjoice* for 'bourgeois'.

Foreigners' English is likewise represented with stereotyped transcriptions. Their pronunciation of *sir* is transcribed *sare*, as in other authors of the same period. Having in his native French no contrast between the vowel of *ranch* and that of *wrench*, the Vicomte de Blissac (*Hot Water*, ch. 3) reports that he had fun on a *cattle-wrench*. In general, however, Wodehouse's foreigners reveal their less-than-perfect command of English in their choice of syntax and vocabulary; their non-English accent is given very little orthographical representation.

5.2. MORPHOLOGY AND SYNTAX

In both inflection[5] and syntax, Wodehouse's narrative prose and the dialogue he puts in the mouth of almost all his characters correspond quite closely to conservative British usage. Once in a while, a somewhat less-than-formal feature of verbal inflection will appear in highly colloquial conversation, as when Lord Bosham and Lady Constance Keeble discuss the Duke of Dunstable's accident (*Uncle Fred in the Springtime*, ch. 12):

"It's true, is it, that the old bird has bust a flipper?"

"He has wrenched his shoulder most painfully," assented Lady Constance, with a happier choice of phrase.

The only fully non-standard deviation from the norm that I have found is the back-formation *glimp*, singular,

from *glimpse*, used by the policeman Harold Potter in
Uncle Dynamite (ch. 13): "I just caught sight of her
for a minute as she legged it away, like as it might have
been a glimp."

In syntax, wherever there is a variation between British and American usage, Wodehouse almost always follows, understandably, the British pattern. Where American English uses the simple form of a verb in the so-
called "subjunctive" construction after verbs referring to
desire, necessity, and the like, British English uses the
inflected form wherever it is available.[6] Thus, in *Uncle
Fred in the Springtime* (ch. 7), Lord Ickenham says:
"It is essential [. . .] that Polly goes to Blandings
and there meets and fascinates Dunstable." (In American
usage, this would be *It is essential that Polly go, meet,
and fascinate.*) After moving permanently to America,
however, Wodehouse began to use the "American subjunctive,"[7] as in the following:

> It was imperative that I be among thost present.
> —*Jeeves and the Feudal Spirit* (ch. 15)
> It was imperative that a wifely pep talk be ad-
> ministered before the coldness of his feet, spreading
> upwards, rendered him incapable of active work.
> —*Pearls, Girls and Monty Bodkin* (ch. 9.3)

There are a few other Briticisms in syntax, as in the
set phrase *out of window* without definite article (*Summer Lightning*, ch. 12.1); the use of *have got* where
American English would use *have* alone *(passim)*; and
the past participle of the pro-verb *do* where American
English would have zero, as in:

> "Did you place that boot there, Smith?"
> "I must have done."
> —*Mike* (ch. 51)
> "Don't you know I've always loved you? [. . .]
> "You can't have done."
> —*Money for Nothing*, ch. 4.ii

"[. . .] my heart bled for you."
"And so it jolly well ought to have done."
—*Stiff Upper Lip, Jeeves*, ch. 7
I could have sworn, indeed, that I didn't drop off
at all, but I suppose I must have done [. . .]'
—*ibid.*, ch. 24.

Occasionally, British English uses prepositions somewhat differently from the way they would be used in
American English, for instance *on the halls* 'in the
vaudeville-theatres' (*Full Moon*, ch. 7.6), or *in Dover
Street (passim)*. The French use of the definite article
with a woman's family name (e.g. *la Bernhardt*—itself
an imitation of the Italian construction *la Duse, il
Machiavelli*) is followed, normally with pejorative connotations, when referring to female characters who are
not liked, e.g. *La Pulbrook* (*The Mating Season*, ch.
22), *La Morehead* (*Jeeves and the Feudal Spirit*, ch. 9),
or *La Briggs* (*Service with a Smile, passim*).

On the morpho-syntactic level, Wodehouse's most
original usage is in the field of word-formation. He
occasionally uses the comparative suffix -*er* and the
superlative suffix -*est* with polysyllabic adjectives,[8]
e.g. *fatheadedest* (*The Mating Season*, ch. 4). Wodehouse often uses the prefix *de*- for new formations, as
when Bertie Wooster speaks of "de-dogging the
premises" (*The Mating Season*, ch. 4), or "de-trousering" some-one (*Frozen Assets*, ch. 10.2). Various suffixes occur in new derivatives, usually of a nonce-kind,
such as the frequent *butlerine; blanc-mange-y* ("Good-
Bye to All Cats"); *beerily* ("Archibald and the Masses");
loopiness (on *loopy* 'crazy'), in all the Uncle Fred
stories; a *nymphery* (*The Mating Season*, ch. 2); or a
self-bearder (*Big Money*, ch. 4):

In short, instead of being a man afflicted by
nature with a beard, and as such more to be pitied
than censured, he was a deliberate putter-on of
beards, a self-bearder, a fellow who, for who knew

what dark reasons, carried his own private jungle around with him, so that at any moment he could dive into it and defy pursuit.

On occasion, Wodehouse uses phrases and clauses as derivational bases in suffixation, such as *fiend-in-human-shape-y* (*Thank You, Jeeves*, ch. 12); *I-wonder-if-this-is-going-to-be-all-right-ness* (*Over Seventy*, ch. 1.2); *Hullo-there-old-boy-how-are-you-ages-since-we-met-ing* (*Cocktail Time*, ch. 2); [. . .] *the aunts raised their eyebrows with a good deal of To-what-are-we-indebted-for-the-honor-of-this-visitness* (*The Mating Season*, ch. 26). Sometimes a word or phrase will be used in the function of another part of speech, as in *I too-badded* (*The Mating Season*, ch. 2).

Occasional nonce-compounds also occur, e.g. formations on *-joy*, such as *pipe-joy* (*Money for Nothing*, ch. 1.ii), *head-joy* 'hats' (*Stiff Upper Lip, Jeeves*, ch. 1), or *lip-joy* 'moustache' (*Jeeves and the Feudal Spirit*, ch. 4), probably in imitation of advertising lingo. Other nonce-compounds include a *coffee-caddie* 'a man [. . .] whose instinct it is to carry his wife's breakfast up to her every morning and bill and coo with her as she wades into it' (*Uncle Dynamite*, ch. 2).[9] Bad suburban architecture can be in the *Neo-Suburbo-Gothic* style (*Big Money*, ch. 5):

> Peacehaven was a two-storey structure in the Neo-Suburbo-Gothic style of architecture, constructed of bricks which appeared to be making a slow recovery from a recent attack of jaundice.

Abbreviations such as *posish* 'position' (*The Code of the Woosters*, ch. 5), *compash* 'compassion' (*ibid.*, ch. 5), or *exclamash* 'exclamation' (*ibid.*, ch. 4.11) are not infrequent.[10]

5.3. LEXICON

A complete concordance to the vocabulary of all Wodehouse's works would undoubtedly reveal a very large number of words of all types, from the most learned and esoteric to the most colloquial. We find such Hellenisms as *callipygous* (*Uncle Dynamite*, ch. 6: "Plainly, he was unwilling to relinquish his memories of a callipygous [Major] Plank"), Latinisms like *diagnostician, assiduously, conciliatory, elephantine, or alleviation;* and Gallicisms like *distrait, insouciance,* or *raisonneur.* Latin tags occur frequently, most of all in Jeeves' conversation, but elsewhere as well, such as *nolle prosequi* or *persona grata.* At the opposite extreme, we find—especially in dialogue—slangy expressions like *oomph* 'feminine charm', *boomps-a-daisy* 'in fine fettle', *dough* 'money' or *chuck out* 'expel'. Many of Wodehouse's colloquialisms are specifically British, and a reader who was not informed of the origin of his books would not find it hard to identify their author as a native speaker of British English, because of such expressions as *the lot* 'all of them [whatever is being referred to]', *be sick* 'vomit', *brass up* 'pay money which is owed', or the frequent pejorative adjective *bally.* Americanisms appear almost exclusively in the speech of his American characters, such as Tipton Plimsoll (*Full Moon; Frozen Assets*), who calls women *dames* and says of Blandings Castle "Some joint!" The comic criminals "Soapy" and Dolly Molloy and "Chimp" Twist use stock Americanisms like *soak* 'hit', *gat* 'revolver', or *pinch* 'arrest'. Occasionally, however, Wodehouse slips up in his Americanisms, e.g. in using *geezer* to refer to some-one other than a cantankerous old man (as when he has *silly little geezer* refer to a child [*Thank You, Jeeves*, ch. 15]).

As a result of the wide range in the types of words which Wodehouse uses, one might expect the syllable-count of his prose to be relatively high.[11] A rough count of two passages from *Full Moon*, one (ch. 2, the first eight paragraphs) consisting wholly of narrative prose, and the other (ch. 6.6, from "Good Lord, Bill!" through "That's the snag") containing almost all dialogue, shows a marked difference between the number of syllables in the two:

	No. of words	Total no. of syllables	No. of syllables per word
Narrative prose	651	964	1.48
Dialogue	653	804	1.23

Furthermore, almost all the three- and four-syllable words in the section containing dialogue occur in the narrative paragraphs connecting the speeches. These proportions bear out the impressionistic judgement which the average reader of Wodehouse is likely to arrive at, that his dialogue is snappy and lively (an impression to which the shortness of the words makes a major contribution), whereas his narrative prose is much fuller of long words. However, Wodehouse does not use any longer words than, say, Henry James (who, in a 782-word passage from *The Ambassadors*, has an average of 1.43 syllables per word) or Mark Twain (who, in 635 words in *Pudd'nhead Wilson*, has a 1.47 average). What saves Wodehouse's narrative prose from heaviness is his unfailing rightness in choosing the *mot juste* (he often refers to Flaubert's search for that elusive desideratum) and his skill in alternating heavy with light vocabulary in the flow of his story-telling.[12]

Notes to Chapter 5

1. One of the major difficulties in presenting objective linguistic analysis to the general public is the almost universal confusion between *language* on the one hand and *style* on the other. The linguistic analyst restricts his use of the former term to the structure of the communicative system (primarily oral-auditory, and only secondarily visual) which humans use in their dealings with each other. He distinguishes sharply between *language*, as defined in this way, and the use which speakers or writers make of it, which is their *style*. Many critics have spoken, for instance, of Wodehouse as "fabricating a new language." No: no individual, not even Dante or Shakespeare, ever "made" or "created" a language. What Dante, Shakespeare, Wodehouse, and every other "creative" writer does, is to develop previously unknown ways of USING the language of his speech-community. This point has been made by many scientific linguists (e.g. Sapir 1922, ch. 11; Bloomfield 1933:21-22; Hockett 1958, ch. 63; Hall 1964b, ch. 69).

2. Cf. Twain's "explanatory" remarks prefaced to *The Adventures of Huckleberry Finn*: "In this book a number of dialects are used, to wit: the Missouri negro dialect; the extremest form of the backwoods Southwestern dialect; the ordinary "Pike County" dialect; and four modified varieties of this last. The shadings have not been done in a haphazard fashion, or by guesswork; but painstakingly, and with the trustworthy guidance and support of personal familiarity with these several forms of speech." Twain did so nevertheless using only the twenty-six letters of the English alphabet. Studies have shown that, by and large, he and other writers who have introduced dialectal matter into their stories have captured perhaps fifty per cent of the characteristics of the speech they were attempting to represent (as pointed out by Tidwell 1947; but cf. also Ives 1950).

3. Cf. Usborne 1961:122.

4. In *Performing Flea* (letter of Sept. 14, 1931), Wodehouse disclaims any ability to write specifically American material.

5. I am of course using the term *inflection* in the sense universally given it in linguistic analysis, i.e. such variations in the form of words as *man—men* or *sing—sang—sung*. The rise and fall in pitch that accompanies speech, often termed "inflection" in popular parlance, is termed *intonation* in linguistics. The term word-formation refers to the derivation of words from other words by such prefixes as *ad-, in-, pre-, post-*, or by such suffices as *-ness, -dom, -ion*, or *-hood*. *Compounding* is the formation of new words by the combination of two or more independent items, as in *spring-time, newspaper,* or *update*.

6. Cf. Fries 1940:103-107.

7. Left as such in the English editions.

8. A procedure which is much more common in every-day English, and especially in conversation, than we are led to believe by puristic grammarians: cf. Alice's *curiouser and curiouser*.

9. Such nonce-formations, also, are far more frequent in ordinary everyday speech than we usually think. Especially with compounds, the widespread habit of avoiding the use of hyphens tends to mask the existence of this type of formation, in marked contrast to, say, German, whose orthography normally writes all compounds as single words.

10. This type of derivation is of course old in English, especially in humorous coinages, some of which have passed from the status of short-lived slang to that of normal vocabulary-items, such as *mob* from *(vulgus)* mob*(ile)* 'the fickle populace', or *bus* from *(omni)bus* '[a vehicle] for all'.

11. In this analysis and that of the number of words per sentence (S 7), I am following the elementary statistical technique suggested by Flesch (1949), as part of a procedure for determining the effectiveness of various styles of writing. It is well known that a free-flowing and maximally effective style in English is correlated with—among other things—short sentences and a low syllable-average per word. (Contrast the "punch" of *The price of liberty is eternal vigilance* with that of *Want to stay free? Keep on your guard all the time!*.)

The figures for James and Twain are from Hall 1969b.

12. This observation applies to the three major types of prose found in Wodehouse: the third-person narrative, the give-and-take of dialogue, and the first-person narrative of Bertie Wooster. As Usborne says a propos of " 'Bertie-Wodehouse' language" (1961:159): "Wodehouse can in Bertie's

artificial language [i.e. style—RAHjr], get from A to B by the shortest route
and still throw all sorts of flowers at your feet as you follow it." Jeeves'
orotund, "Augustan" manner is of course intentionally aberrant, with a
much higher syllable-count per word—and, for that matter, a much higher
word-count per sentence.

6

Stylistic Devices

6.1. THE NATURE OF COMIC STYLISTIC DEVICES

The SD's commonly used in serious writing are of the kind that tend to elevate the level of discourse. In morphology, for instance, an archaic plural like *kine* or a verb-form in *-eth* will immediately evoke poetic connotations for a present-day speaker of English. In syntax, we ascribe lofty, noble associations to variations from our current every-day usage such as the prolepsis (placing out in front of the sentence) of an adverbial element; the direct postposition of an adjectival modifier of a noun; the inversion of subject and verb or of verb and object; and the use of the auxiliary *do* with a verb (instead of the normal verb alone) in non-emphatic, non-interrogative sentences. These four syntactic SD's are exemplified in the first five lines of Coleridge's *Kubla Khan*:[1]

> IN XANADU DID Kubla Khan
> A stately PLEASURE-DOME DECREE
> Where Alph, the sacred river, ran
> Through caverns MEASURELESS TO MAN
> Down to a sunless sea.

In lexicon, likewise, certain words and set phrases have special connotations because of their use in particularly prestigious writings (especially, in English, the King James Bible or Shakespeare), such as *to*

79

flourish like the green bay-tree, the salt of the earth,
or *the slings and arrows of outrageous fortune.* In addition, just as in morphology and syntax, some lexical
items are archaic, poetical, or dialectal, and evoke
special associations: *vagrom, ere, list* 'wish, desire', or
Hist!. In general, moreover, serious writers seek after con-
gruity, an over-all harmony between the various elements of their discourse. The average reader is dis-
turbed if, in a serious work, the author introduces dis-
parate features which mar its sustained tone.[2]

Humor, on the other hand, has two essential in-
gredients. For us to laugh at something, it must contain some kind of incongruity, and we must be
emotionally neutral, without our personal feelings being
involved. The effect of incongruity is to lead the hearer
or reader "up the garden path," inducing him to expect one resolution, on the basis of what he has been
told up to a certain point, and then to present him
with a development quite different from what he has
expected, as in the old joke *What should you do to
make ice last?—Prepare everything else first.*[3] The
absence of emotional involvement is essentially what
Fry (1963) calls the "play-frame" within which jokes
are funny, the recognition that it is "all in fun" and not
to be taken in earnest. (Compare, for instance, the effect
which Stan Laurel's dropping a pile of plates, in a
Laurel and Hardy comedy, has on us, with what we feel
if we ourselves do the same thing in real life.)

Wodehouse makes use of just about every resource
available in standard English, plus a few from non-
standard English, to obtain his effects of incongruity,
tickling the reader's risibilities. I shall take up, first his
structural (phonological, morpho-syntactic) SD's, then
those based on features of lexicon, and finally those
involving the level of discourse (including cliches and
literary allusions).

6.2 PHONOLOGICAL DEVICES

Relatively little of Wodehouse's humor is based upon features of the phonology of standard British English. Occasional puns are based upon the replacement of *r* by length (of a preceding vowel), which creates pairs of homonyms such as *ma* and *mar*, *pa* and *par* in British English. At one point (*The Mating Season*, ch. 8), Bertie Wooster asks Jeeves:

> "What's that thing of Shakespeare's about some-
> one having an eye like Mother's?"
> "An eye like Mars, to threaten and command, is
> possibly the quotation for which you are groping,
> sir."

The habit of abbreviating *thank you* to '*k you* is re-flected in Wodehouse's use of the homonymous letter *Q* in *San the Sudden* (ch. 2), when we first meet Kay Derrick as she is booking a ticket on the top of a London bus:

> "Fez pliz."
> "Valley Fields," said Kay.
> "Q."

Misplaced stress, in Albert Peasemarch's formal sub-standard, can result in such forms as *intricket* for *intricate*, and *Bandollero* for *Bandolero* (the name of a song), each presumably stressed on the second syllable.

We have already mentioned (S 5.1) Wodehouse's oc-casional use of features of American English, most of which would seem, in themselves, mildly funny to speakers of British English. The contrast between the two is utilised when, after quarrelling with her Ameri-can fiance Tubby Vanringham over his accent, Pru-dence Whittaker (in *Summer Moonshine*, ch. 26), at the height of her anger against the villainess, Princess von und zu Dwornitschek, finds that nothing will do to ex-press her contempt but the Americanism "Ah, nerts!"

Rustic English speech enters but rarely into Wodehouse's phonological humor; the only example that
comes readily to mind is Bill Lister's use of stylized
mock-rustic speech (*Full Moon*, ch. 6), when he is disguised as a gardener at Blandings and has been engaged in conversation with Lord Emsworth:

> He had fought off the challenge with a masterly
> series of "yes, m'lords" and "Ah, m'lords" and once
> an inspired "Ah, that du zurely be zo, m'lord" [. . .].

Occasionally, one of Wodehouse's characters will attempt to reproduce a phrase in a foreign language, with
only partial success, as does Albert Peasemarch (*The
Luck of the Bodkins*) in his use of such tags as *see
jewness savvay* 'si jeunesse savait' and *fam fatarl* 'femme
fatale'. In *French Leave*, the American publisher
Russell Clutterbuck is continually referring to the
maquis as the *macky*.

Most of Wodehouse's non-native speakers of English
are Frenchmen, whose attempts at using English include
such phonological reshapings as *Zoosmeet* for *Shoesmith* (*Frozen Assets*, ch. 1 ff.). Wodehouse's own supposed or real ignorance of a foreign language can be
turned to account, as when he describes the behavior of
a Swede who has dived into New York harbor (*The Girl
on the Boat*, ch. 2.3):

> "Svensk!" exclaimed Mr. Swenson, or whatever
> it is that natives of Sweden exclaim in moments of
> annoyance.

He also makes up imaginary African languages and gives
mock translations of them, as in "The Bishop's Move":

> His unerring acumen had won for him from the
> natives the sobriquet of Wah-nah-B'gosh-B'jingo—
> which, freely translated, means Big Chief Who Can
> See Through The Hole In A Doughnut.

Here, of course, the mock-African closely resembles the
English exclamations "What now! By gosh! By jingo!"
Among minor phonological phenomena may be in-
cluded an occasional humorous interpretation of ono-
matopoeia, as in "Lord Emsworth and the Girl Friend":

"Glug!" said Lord Emsworth—which, as any
philologist will tell you, is the sound which peers
of the realm make when stricken to the soul while
drinking coffee.

When spiritually aroused, Bertie Wooster is likely to
perpetrate spoonerisms and similar slips of the tongue,
such as *Jumenfeld Blunior* for "Blumenfeld junior"
("Jeeves and the Dog McIntosh"), or "Tup, Tushy!—
I mean, Tush, Tuppy!" (*Right Ho, Jeeves*, ch. 12).
Very little purely orthographical humor is present
in Wodehouse's writing, the only outstanding example
being his play with the British habit of writing certain
aristocratic proper names with lower-case *ff—* instead of
upper-case *F—*, in "A Slice of Life":

"Sir Jasper Finch-Farrowmere?" said Wilfred.
"ffinch-ffarowmere," corrected the visitor, his
sensitive ears detecting the capital letters.

6.3. MORPHOLOGICAL AND SYNTACTIC DEVICES

We have already mentioned (S 5.2) the forms *glimp*
(a back-formation on *glimpse*) and *bust* as being among
the rare bits of inflectional humor in Wodehouse's
dialogue. In "Jeeves and the Yuletide Spirit," Sir
Roderick Glossop misunderstands Bertie Wooster's
use of the nick-name *Tuppy*:

"Awfully sorry about all this," I said in a hearty
sort of voice. "The fact is, I thought you were Tuppy."
"Kindly refrain from inflicting your idiotic slang

on me. What do you mean by the adjective 'tuppy'?"
"It isn't so much an adjective, don't you know.
More of a noun, I should think, if you examine it
squarely. What I mean to say is, I thought you were
your nephew."

Somewhat more frequent are the inventive word-
formations with prefixes and suffixes. To *de-dog the
premises* (*The Mating Season*, ch. 24) is not too great a
variation on the pattern of *de-louse* or *de-bunk*; but
Wodehouse obtains a greater humorous effect by pre-
fixing *de-* to proper names, as when Pongo Twistleton
brings the house-maid Elsie Bean out of a cupboard
(*Uncle Dynamite*, ch. 9): "His manner as he de-Beaned
the cupboard was somewhat distrait," or when "Kipper"
Herring, after Bobbie Wickham has left his company, is
described as "finding himself de-Wickhamed" (*Jeeves
in the Offing*, ch. 14). On the analogy of such formations as *homeward, northward, inward*, Wodehouse
obtains a special effect when he says of Lord Emsworth
"He pottered off pigward" (*Summer Lightning*, ch.
1.ii).[1]
Specifically humorous, because they stretch the pat-
terns of word-formation well beyond their normal limits, are such back-formations as the verb *huss* on the
noun *hussy* (*Heavy Weather*, ch. 6):

"I regard the entire personnel of the ensemble
of our musical comedy theatres as—if you will par-
don me being Victorian for a moment—painted
hussies."
"They've got to paint."
"Well, they needn't huss."

We also find the "neglected positives" *gruntled* and
couth:

I could see that, if not actually disgruntled, he
was far from being gruntled.
                          —*The Code of the Woosters*, ch. 1

He interrupted me with the uncouth abruptness
so characteristic of these human gorillas. Roderick
Spode may have had his merits [. . .] but his
warmest admirer couldn't have called him couth.
—*Stiff Upper Lip, Jeeves*, ch. 13

What does a cow puncher do? Obviously he punches
cows (*Uncle Dynamite*, ch. 4), and of a corn-chandler,
Bertie Wooster says (*Right Ho, Jeeves*, ch. 17) "He was
looking a bit fagged, I thought, as if he had had a hard
morning chandling the corn." In one instance, a Wodehouse character separates *hobnob* into its constituent
elements (*Uncle Dynamite*, ch. 8):

It all depended on what you meant by the expression [i.e. *hobnob*]. To offer a housemaid a
cigarette is not hobbing. Nor, when you light it
for her, does that constitute nobbing.

In the same novel, Lord Ickenham asks Bill Oakshott to
testify to "the hundred per cent Twistletonity" of Pongo
Twistleton (ch. 9.1).

In syntax, Lord Emsworth's inability to grasp the
meaning of Gladys's *flarze* 'flowers' (cf. § 5.1) leads him
to interpret it as a mass-noun ("Lord Emsworth and the
Girl Friend"):

"Could 'e 'ave some flarze?"
"Certainly," said Lord Emsworth. "Certainly,
certainly, certainly. By all means. Just what I was
about to suggest my—er—what *is* flarze?"
Beach, the linguist, intervened.
"I think the young lady means flowers, your lord-
ship."

We find a mock passive in *Brass rags had been parted
by the young couple* (*The Code of the Woosters*, ch. 6).

The "pivot-construction," whose humor depends on a
given word being used as the center, first of an expression with literal meaning and then of another hav-

ing an idiomatic or metaphorical sense, is rare in Wodehouse. The only instance I have found is "He was in
evening dress and hysterics" (Not George Washington,
ch. 18).

Parallel constructions are sometimes used, with resultant incongruous contradictions, as in "The Luck of
the Stiffhams":

> "You look as if you had seen a ghost."
> "I have seen a ghost."
> "The White Lady of Wivelscombe?"
> "No, the Pink Secretary of Wivelscombe."

Not infrequently—but not with excessive frequency,
either, perhaps once or twice in any given story—Wodehouse uses what is termed in rhetoric the "transferred
epithet," especially an adjective modifying a noun instead of the corresponding adverb modifying the verb
of the sentence:

> He was now smoking a sad cigarette and waiting
> for the blow to fall.
> —Uneasy Money (1917), ch. 9
> He uncovered the fragrant eggs and I pronged a
> moody forkful.
> —"Jeeves and the Impending Doom" (ca. 1926)
> Such, then, is the sequence of events which
> led up to Bertram Wooster [. . .] standing at the
> door [. . .] through the aromatic smoke of a
> meditative cigarette.
> —Thank You, Jeeves (1934), ch. 2
> It was the hottest day of the summer, and though
> somebody had opened a tentative window or two,
> the atmosphere remained distinctive and individual.
> —Right Ho, Jeeves (1934), ch. 17
> I balanced a thoughtful lump of sugar on the
> teaspoon.
> —Joy in the Morning (1946), ch. 5
> He waved a concerned cigar.
> —Jeeves and the Feudal Spirit (1954), ch. 11

> Lord Ickenham proceeded to Beach's pantry
> where, with a few well-chosen words, he slipped a
> remorseful five-pound note into the other's hand.
> —*Service with a Smile* (1962), ch. 7
> Jerry [. . .] took a moody spoonful of marma-
> lade
> —*Frozen Assets* (1964), ch. 2.4

(In these examples, I have given the dates of the stories,
to emphasize that this SD is found from Wodehouse's
earliest to his most recent work.) As I have pointed out
elsewhere,[5] the basis of this syntactic procedure is
essentially semantic, referring to emotions or attitudes
on the part of some person as expressed by a physical
action, expression, or characteristic. When the epithet is
transferred, we have simply an incongruous extension
of the type of reference involved in non-transferred·
epithets such as *He shimmered out, and I took another listless stab at the e[ggs] and b[acon]* ("Jeeves
and the Impending Doom"): In at least one instance,
Wodehouse pushes the use of the transferred epithet
one step further, bringing it into direct relation to the
grammatical subject of the sentence, but preserving its
reference to the emotions of the person immediately
concerned:

> It was plain that I had shaken him. His eyes
> widened, and an astonished piece of toast fell from
> his grasp.
> —*Jeeves in the Offing* (1960), ch. 2

Syntactic and lexical ambiguities can give rise to
misunderstandings and resultant comic cross-talk, as
when Constable Potter confuses *by* indicating agent
with *by* 'near' (*Uncle Dynamite*, ch. 13):

> "I was assaulted by the duck pond."
> "By the duck pond?" Sir Aylmer asked, his eyes
> widening.

"Yes, sir."

"How the devil can you be assaulted by a duck pond?"

ﾉ ｽtable Potter saw where the misunderstanding had arisen. The English language is full of these pitfalls.

"When I say 'by the duck pond,' I didn't mean 'by the duck pond,' I meant 'by the duck pond.' That is to say," proceeded Constable Potter, speaking just in time, " 'near' or adjacent to', in fact 'on the edge of'."

Similarly, in "The Amazing Hat Mystery," Percy Wimbolt interprets Nelson Cork's use of *abroad* as meaning 'in foreign parts', rather than 'in the land':

"There is lawlessness and licence abroad."

"And here in England too."

"Well, naturally, you silly ass," said Nelson, with some asperity. "When I said abroad, I didn't mean abroad, I meant abroad."

An ambiguity in pronominal reference can lead to cross-talk like that between Bertie Wooster and Pauline Stoker:

"At nine tomorrow morning he will bring me tea."

"Well, you'll like that."

"He will bring it to this room. He will approach the bed. He will put it on this table."

"What on earth for?"

"To facilitate my getting at the cup and sipping."

"Oh, you mean he will put the tea on the table. You said he would put the bed on the table."

—*Thank You, Jeeves*, ch. 7

Compare the confusion which Leonard Q. Ross's Hyman Kaplan gets into when he tells some-one "If your eye falls on a bargain, pick it up."

6.4 LEXICAL DEVICES

Most of Wodehouse's SD's involve play with lexical items and their semantic fields. He often uses terms out of their normal contexts, especially learned words in non-learned environments, as when Lord Emsworth is described as he reads a new book on the care of pigs (*A Pelican at Blandings*, ch. 10):

> He had to read on to see how it all came out in the end, and, in so doing, he arrived at Chapter Five and the passage about the newly-discovered vitamin pill for stimulating the porcine appetite.

An irate house-owner in *Big Money* (ch. 6) replaces *bloody* (a taboo-word in British English) with comically learned synonyms:

> "I catch you in my hall, sneaking my ensanguined hats, and you have the haemorrhagic insolence to stand there and tell me it's quite all right!"

At the opposite extreme, markedly colloquial expressions will occur in the midst of very formal discourse:

> There is an expression in common use which might have been invented to describe the enterprising peer in moments such as this: the expression "boomps-a-daisy." You could look askance at his methods, you could shake your head at him in disapproval and click your tongue in reproof, but you could not deny that he was boomps-a-daisy.
> —*Uncle Dynamite*, ch. 5

> Well, two weeks ago, it seems, they had blown up one of the Hall's Elizabethan oaks and as near as a toucher, Rudge learned, had blown up Colonel Wyvern and Mr. Carmody with it.
> —*Money for Nothing*, ch. 1.i

> What with being hopelessly in love and one thing and another, his soul was in rather a bruised condition these days, and he found himself deriving from the afternoon placidity of Rudge-in

the-Vale a certain balm and consolation.
                                        —*ibid.*, ch. 1.ii

Often, an exaggerated synonym will make us smile, as when Wodehouse says of Lord Emsworth (*A Pelican at Blandings*, ch. 10) "To a sensitive man, the spectacle of a cascade of people falling downstairs is always disturbing." Of Esmond Haddock's five aunts, Bertie Wooster says "As far as the eye could reach, I found myself gazing on a surging sea of aunts." In describing the village of Rudge-in-the-Vale, Wodehouse tells us:

> Quiet—in fact, almost unconscious—it nestles by the tiny river Skirme and lets the world go by [. . .].
> —*Money for Nothing*, ch. 1.i

Sometimes we find a pair of synonyms in succession, the second one exaggerating the first, as when Lord Ickenham asks "What have you been doing, Bill Oakshott, to merit this reception—nay, this durbar?" (*Uncle Dynamite*, ch. 2).

In narrative passages, Wodehouse does not shun quite a high level of learned connotation in choice of lexicon. A large proportion of the humorous effects of his narrative comes from the ease with which he moves—from one sentence, one phrase, and even one word to the next—between the formal and the informal level, as in the well-known beginning of *The Luck of the Bodkins*:

> Into the face of the young man who sat on the terrace of the Hotel Magnifique at Cannes there had crept a look of furtive shame, the shifty, hangdog look which announces that an Englishman is about to talk French.

As far as the first comma, this might be the beginning of a serious novel; but the sudden colloquialisms *shifty* and *hangdog* prepare us, by a change of lexical level, for the semantic incongruity of the last part of the sentence. (For a detailed analysis of this and the following material in *The Luck of the Bodkins*, cf. § 7.)

When Wodehouse tells a story in the first person, putting it in the mouth of one of his characters it is usually on the exact cultural level that would be expected of the person involved. His most frequently used first-person narrator, Bertie Wooster, began in the period from 1915 to 1930 as a breezy, amiable, cheerful, but (despite his Eton and Oxford training) wholly unintellectual young man-about-town, with a correspondingly colloquial, free-and-easy narrative style. In the novels about Bertie and Jeeves, beginning with *Thank You, Jeeves* (1934), even Bertie's style (particularly vocabulary) comes to be considerably more formal, not shunning such decidedly learned words as *acerbity, dubious, pulchritude,* or *staccato.* Bertie specifically ascribes this improvement in his vocabulary to Jeeves' influence (*Thank You, Jeeves,* ch. 4):

> "Where do you pick up these expressions?"
> "Well, I suppose from Jeeves, mostly. My late man. He had a fine vocabulary."

Bertie's and his friends' fishing for recondite items of vocabulary is frequently a source of humor, as when he is speaking to Jeeves in *The Mating Season* (ch. 8):

> "Then what we've got to do is to strain every nerve to see that he makes a hit. What are those things people have?"
> "Sir?"
> "Opera singers and people like that."
> "You mean a claque, sir?"
> "That's right. The word was on the tip of my tongue."

Elsewhere, Bertie says:

I had a . . . what's the word? . . . begins with
a p . . . pre-something . . . presentiment, that's
the baby [. . .].
                                  —*Stiff Upper Lip, Jeeves*, ch. 2
"[. . .] I suppose Stiffy's sore about this . . .
what's the word? . . . Not vaseline . . . Vacil-
lation, that's it."
                                                          —*ibid.*, ch. 3.
"Let a plugugly like young Thos loose in the
community with a cosh, and you are inviting
disasters and . . . what's the word? Something
about cats."
    "Cataclysms, sir?"
    "That's it. Cataclysms."
                              —*Jeeves and the Feudal Spirit*, ch. 16
I knew what was stopping him getting action.
It was not . . . it's on the tip of my tongue . . .
begins with a p . . . I've heard Jeeves use the word
. . . pusillanimity, that's it, meaning broadly that
a fellow is suffering from a pronounced case of
cold feet [. . .]
                                  —*Stiff Upper Lip, Jeeves*, ch. 15

Stiffy Byng gets confused between a London moving-
firm, a dime-novel detective, and a Dickens hero in *The
Code of the Woosters* (ch. 13):

    "You remind me of Carter Paterson—no, that's
    not it—Nick Carter—no, not Nick Carter—Who
    does Mr. Wooster remind me of, Jeeves?"
    "Sydney Carton, miss."

On occasion, Wodehouse has Bertie excuse his choice
of phraseology by a semi-apologetic "if that's the word
I want," "as the fellow said," or "as Jeeves says." Only
Jeeves (and, to a lesser extent, the pompous-ass psychi-
atrist Sir Roderick Glossop) speaks in a continuously
lofty, ultra-formal manner, with lengthy sentences and
a high proportion of learned terms. Jeeves puts the
American tycoon Mr. Stoker in his place by snowing

him under with ultra-formal parlance (*Thank You, Jeeves*, ch. 18):

> "England is an extremely law-abiding country, sir, and offences which might pass unnoticed in your own land are prosecuted here with the greatest rigour. My knowledge of legal minutiae is, I regret to say, slight, so I cannot asseverate with perfect confidence that this detention of Mr. Wooster would have ranked as an act in contravention of the criminal code, and, as such, liable to punishment with penal servitude, but undoubtedly, had I not intervened, the young gentleman would have been in a position to bring a civil action and mulct you in very substantial damages."

Sometimes, therefore, Bertie has to translate for the benefit of those who are less familiar with Jeeves' learned expatiations, as in "The Artistic Career of Corky":

> "The scheme I would suggest cannot fail of success, but it has what may seem to you a drawback, sir, in that it requires a certain financial outlay."
> "He means," I translated to Corky, "that he has got a pippin of an idea, but it's going to cost a lot."

The unexpected use of a continuously high-flown, ultra-formal narrative style, with the only contrast coming in Bertie's conversation, is the stylistic main-spring of Jeeves' telling the story of "Bertie Changes His Mind" in the first person, rather than Bertie's doing so, as is the case in the other stories about the two.

After he started writing for the American market, Wodehouse used more specifically British lexical items for humorous effect than he had previously. The stories of the 1920's dealing with the Drones Club and its members contain a number of Briticisms such as *bird* 'girl, woman', *bar* 'draw the line at, object to', *get into the ribs of* 'touch for money', *loony-bin* 'insane-asylum', *in my puff* 'in my life', *come unstuck* 'go amiss', *be all over some-one* 'be enthusiastic about some-one', *cove* (also *bloke, chappie*) 'fellow'; *blighter* or *rotter* 'objectionable person', *rannygazoo* 'ruction, disturbance', *oojah-cum-spiff* 'as well as could be desired', or such expressions of farewell as *bung-oh, teuf-teuf, tinkerty-tonk, pip-pip,* or *toodle-oo.*[6] Closely allied to this somewhat affected way of talking was the use of exaggerated synonyms to vary one's conversation, as when Bertie Wooster or others speak of *toddling* around or *squashing in* with the domestic staff (*Uncle Fred in the Springtime,* ch. 8). In the first story in which Bertie appears ("Extricating Young Gussie"), his Aunt Agatha expresses her strong disapproval of this manner of speaking:

> "What are your immediate plans, Bertie?"
> "Well, I rather thought of tottering out for a bite of lunch later on, and then possibly staggering round to the club, and after that, if I felt strong enough, I might trickle off to Walton Heath for a round of golf."
> "I am not interested in your totterings and tricklings."

This use of exaggerated synonyms is pushed even farther in two ways: reference to words (which are obvious from the context) by their initial letters alone, and metonymy based on identity of minor semantic features. Bertie Wooster is especially given to the first of these procedures:

> I emitted a hollow g.
> —*Thank You Jeeves,* ch. 12
> [Sir Roderick Glossop is being kept prisoner in a shed:["Can you remove Sir R. from the s., Jeeves?"
> —*ibid.,* ch. 21
> "Paddington!" he shouted to the charioteer, and was gone with the wind, leaving me gaping after him, all of a twitter.

And I'll tell you why I was all of a t.
                    —*Stiff Upper Lip, Jeeves*, ch. 3, 4
As I stood there gaping at that closed door, a
vision rose before my eyes, featuring me and an
inspector of police [. . .].
Such was the v. that rose before my e., as I gazed at
that c.d.
                    —*Jeeves and the Feudal Spirit*, ch. 19

Wodehouse's characters not infrequently use re-
cherché synonyms (often phrases instead of single
words), based on far-fetched comparisons.[7] Psmith is
especially given to this procedure, but Bertie Wooster
and other Wodehouse characters also use it. They are
continually referring to a cup of tea as *a cup of the
steaming*, which refreshes one by *restoring the tissues*.
A person who is low psychologically might be said to
be "in the cellar," and from this comparison is described
as *down among the wines and spirits* (with, perhaps,
also an oblique reference to the expression *down in
spirit*). When Psmith wants to ask Mike where he
"hangs out," he asks him "Where are you suspended
at present?" (*Psmith in the City*, ch. 7).
Malapropisms are rare in Wodehouse, and occur almost exclusively in the speech of the ship's steward
Albert Peasemarch (*The Luck of the Bodkins*). We have
already mentioned his *copperising* 'compromising' and
undeliable 'indelible', and his mis-stressing of *intricket*
'intricate' and *Bandollero* 'Bandolero'. He is unable
to *veridify* whether a state-room has been *vacatuated*.
He also refers to an *argle-bargle* or *imbroglio* as an
imbrolligo, and remarks philosophically "what help-
less prawns [pawns] we are in the clutches of a remorse-
less fate" (ch. 18). He recurs again in *Cocktail Time*,
but in the later book he does not perpetrate any further
malapropisms and is a much more sympathetic character than in *The Luck of the Bodkins*. In *The Old
Reliable*, one of the personages is said to be *as rich as
Creosote*. Bertie Wooster twice uses *incredulous* for

incredible (*The Code of the Woosters*, ch. 5; *Stiff Upper Lip, Jeeves*, ch. 5).

Puns are not infrequent; they are always apposite, though not always subtle. Lord Ickenham, while masquerading as Major Brabazon-Plank, gets his hearers all confused by a lengthy disquisition on himself as Brabazon-Plank *major* (i.e. the elder), a *miner* by profession, as opposed to an imaginary brother who is *minor* (i.e. younger) but a *major* in the army (Uncle Dynamite, ch. 7). Among other puns, we may cite:

> [Jeeves has just given notice:]
> "No, sir. I fear I cannot recede from my position."
> "But, dash it, you say you are receding from your position."
> "I should have said, I cannot abandon the stand which I have taken."
> *—Thank You, Jeeves*, ch. 1
> "Mr. Stoker [. . .] is enquiring after Miss Stoker's whereabouts."
> Well, of course, there's always the old one about them being at the wash, but this seemed to me neither the time nor the place.
> *—ibid.*, ch. 5
> "Reminds me of that thing about Lo somebody's name led all the rest."
> Jeeves coughed. He had that informative gleam of his in his eyes.
> "Abou ben Adhem, sir."
> "Have I *what?*" said old Stoker, puzzled.
> *—ibid.*, ch. 21
> "Oh, ah, yes, of course, definitely." I remembered something Jeeves had once called Gussie. "A sensitive plant, what?"
> "Exactly. You know your Shelley, Bertie."
> "Oh, am I?"
> *—The Code of the Woosters*, ch. 3
> "I look like something the cat found in Tutankhamen's tomb, do I not?"
> "I would not go as far as that, sir, but I have unquestionably seen you more *soigné*."

It crossed my mind for an instant that with a little thought one might throw together something rather clever about "Way down upon the soigné river," but I was too listless to follow up.

—*The Mating Season*, ch. 20

[After Bertie has spent a night in jail:]

"Are you all right now?"

"Well, I have a pinched look."

—*Jeeves and the Feudal Spirit*, ch. 6

"What was that about glue?"

"Igloo. It's a sort of gloo they have up in the Arctic circle."

"I see."

"Stickier than the usual kind."

—*The Old Reliable*, ch. 4

"It won't be long," said the girl, "before Wilberforce suddenly rises in the world."

She never spoke a truer word. At this very moment, up he came from behind the settee like a leaping salmon.

—"Uncle Fred Flits By"

"They're sitting in my parlor as cool as dammit, swigging my tea and buttered toast."

"I thought as much."

"And they've opened a pot of my raspberry jam."

"Ah, they you will be able to catch them red-handed."

—*ibid.*

The story "Noblesse Oblige" depends on the identity in pronunciation between French *mille* 'thousand (-franc-note)' and English *meal*:

"But you said you had to have a *mille*."

"And a meal is just what I am going to have," replied the chap, enthusiastically.

Mis-hearings can give rise to comic cross-talk, as when Pauline Stoker tells Bertie Wooster (*Thank You, Jeeves,* ch. 4):

"That's the comfort of having been engaged to a man. When you break it off, you feel such a sister."
"I don't regard you as a blister at all," I said warmly. "You had a perfect right . . ."
"Not blister. Sister!"
"Oh, sister? You mean, you look on me as a brother."
"Yes, as a brother. How quick you are."

Foreign loans are fairly frequent—chiefly French words and phrases, virtually all prestigious, of the type of *macedoine; truite bleue; espièglerie; noblesse oblige; preux chevalier; joie de vivre; bonhomie* (which serves as a base for the derived adjective *bonhomous); raissonneur; tête-a-tête; reculer pour mieux sauter; l'audace, toujours l'audace;* etc. They are mostly used seriously, but are sometimes found in incongruous contexts, e.g. *mésalliance* applied to a convict's sister marrying a policeman (*Uncle Dynamite,* ch. 3.5). Jeeves often interlards his disquisitions with Latin tags such as *nolle prosequi* or *rem acu tetigisti.* Part of the time, Bertie does not understand them, but, especially in the later books, shows himself an apt pupil by using them himself in the appropriate context.

Interestingly enough, Wodehouse's foreigners do not use much of their native languages, apart from an occasional phrase in the mouth of, say, Anatole (Bertie's Aunt Dahlia's French cook), who says such things as "Je me fiche de ce type infect. C'est idiot de faire comme ça l'oiseau. Allez-vous-en, louffier!" (*Right Ho, Jeeves,* ch. 20). For the most part, the humor in their speech comes from their hashed-up English, with such curiosities as the French hotel-keeper's "Yes, by damn! [. . .] You give my hotel bad names, would you or wasn't it?" ("Pearls Mean Tears"). The most extensive linguistic mixture in Wodehouse's English-as-spoken-by-Frenchmen is the combination of colloquial British and American usage with real or imaginary loan-translations from French in Anatole's speech. His longest diatribe is in *Right Ho, Jeeves* (ch. 20, here cited only in part):

> "Hot dog! You ask me what is it? Listen. Make some attention a little. Me, I have hit the hay, but I do not sleep so good, and presently I wake and up I look, and there is one who makes faces against me through the dashed window. [. . .] If you think I like it, you jolly well mistake yourself. I am so mad as a wet hen. And why not? I am somebody, isn't it? And why not? This is a bedroom, what-what, not a house for some apes? Then for what do blighters sit on my window as cool as a few cucumbers, making some faces [. . .]? I am not content with such folly. I think the poor mutt's loony."

In "The Clicking of Cuthbert," the Russian novelist Vladimir Brusiloff (who "gave the impression that each word was excavated from his interior by some up-to-date process of mining") delivers his dicta in a somewhat stylized broken English with the equational (verbless) clause as its only Russian-like feature:

> "No novelists any good except me. Sovietski—yah! Nastikoff—bah! I spit me of zem all. No novelists anywhere any good except me. P. G. Wodehouse and Tolstoi not bad. Not good, but not bad. No novelists any good except me."

The names which Wodehouse gives his characters and his imaginary firms, places, and brands of goods are one of his prime sources of humor.[8] Probably the majority of his characters have every-day names like Nelson Cork, Richard Little, or Harold Potter, but many have names with some special connotation. The arty young men of the extensive Mulliner trible have first names which suggest the Sitwell family, e.g. Sacheverell or Osbert, or Tennysonian names like Mordred or Lancelot. Another, named to commemorate the event which brought his father and mother together, is John San Francisco Earthquake Mulliner ("The Story of William"). In *Jeeves and the Feudal Spirit*, a Liverpool business-man is named Lemuel Gengulphus Trotter, a fact which militates against his wanting to be knighted (when he would have to be called Sir Lemuel). Once in a while, a character's given name or family-name or both will reflect his nature or his role in the story as when the aggressive, threatening rival of Osbert Mulliner is named J. Bashford Braddock ("The Ordeal of Osbert Mulliner").[9] The hero of "The Heart of a Goof" is Ferdinand Dibble.[10] More often, the names of some of Wodehouse's characters simply have secondary associations,[11] for instance the barber George Christopher Meech (in *If I Were You*), who had been engaged for eight and a half years and was beginning to talk about getting married (ch. 12); the American publisher Russell Clutterbuck (*French Leave*); the movie-producers Sigismund Glutz and Jacob Z. Schnellenhamer; or the butler Augustus Keggs. The name of Captain Biggar (in *Ring for Jeeves*) lends itself to a whole series of jokes, such as "Which is bigger, Captain Biggar or Mrs. Biggar?—Mrs. Biggar, because she became bigger." Gussie Fink-Nottle makes himself so obnoxious to Bertie Wooster's Aunt Dahlia that she resolves to call him henceforth Spink-Bottle, an obvious euphemism replacing a very similar word in the first part (*Right Ho, Jeeves*, ch. 19).

A humorously aristocratic flavor is found in the names of many of the members of the Drones Club, such as Algernon, Archibald, Augustus, Bertram, Cyril, Hildebrand, Mortimer, Percy, or Reginald. (Curiously, at the very end of his fictional career, Jeeves' first name is revealed to be Reginald.) Middle names, also, are often aristocratic or pseudo-aristocratic, e.g. Frederick Fotheringay (pronounced "Fungy") Widgeon, Stanley Featherstonehaugh (pronounced "Fanshaw") Ukridge, Thomas Portarlington Travers, Cuthbert Gervase Brabazon Biggar, or Claude Cattermole Potter-Pirbright (whose nickname "Catsmeat" reflects both his middle name and the first part of his surname). Nicknames, however, are markedly colloquial, for instance "Pongo" Twistleton, "Bingo" Little, "Beefy" Bingham, "Tuppy" Glossop, or "Stilton" Cheesewright. Especially the older, more dignified men often have singularly inappropriate, discourteous nicknames dating from their school-years, such as Sir Aylmer ("Mugsy") Bostock, Sir Roderick ("Pimples") Glossop, Major ("Bimbo") Brabazon-Plank, George ("Stinker") Pyke (Lord Tilbury), and Frederick Altamont Cornwallis ("Barmy")[12] Twistleton (lord Ickenham). Most of Wodehouse's girl-characters have straightforward names like Anne, Jane, Prudence, or Myrtle, with equally straightforward nicknames like Kay, Sue, or Sally. Only a few eccentric girls have more unusual nicknames such as Cora ("Corky") Pirbright (*The Mating Season*); Stephanie ("Stiffy") Byng (*The Code of the Woosters* and *Stiff Upper Lip, Jeeves*); or Zenobia ("Nobby") Hopwood (*Joy in the Morning*). Cf. Usborne's observations (1961: 163), quoted in § 3.2, note 10.

Many of Wodehouse's family-names are more or less comical in their own right, like Twistleton, Pilbeam, Peasemarch, Bodkin, Worple, or Poskitt, even if they have no clearly definable associations. Certain names seem to have appealed to Wodehouse for their humorous value as applied to butlers, chauffeurs, and policemen, and we find Bulstrode, Voules, and Meadowes repeatedly given to such characters. In England, anmes like Higginbotham are often thought of as typically American, and so some of Wodehouse's American tycoons have names like J. Felkin Haggenbaker (*Sam the Sudden*), J. Chichester Clam (*Joy in the Morning*), J. Wellington Gedge (*Hot Water*)—note the recurrence of the initial J. in the first-name-slot—and T[orquil] Paterson Frisby (*Big Money*). His noblemen often have the names of small towns (often but not always in the south of England) or of London suburbs, e.g. Lord Ickenham, Lord Emsworth, or the Duke of Dunstable. Some names give humorous effects in pronunciation, such as Freddie Widgeon's uncle Lord Blicester (= *blister*) in "Noblesse Oblige," "The Fat of the Land," etc., or Lord Rowcester (= *roaster*) in *Ring for Jeeves*.[13] One of the most popular of Wodehouse's earlier characters is Ronald Eustace Psmith, who deliberately adopted the spelling with the silent *p* "as in pshrimp" (*Leave It to Psmith*, ch. 5). Probably his most famous character is Jeeves, who, Wodehouse tells us,[14] was named after a well-known cricketer of the turn of the century, on the theory that characters named after popular cricketers were likely to be successful.

In naming imaginary places, Wodehouse gives full play to his inventiveness, producing such masterpieces of incongruity as Wockley Junction, Eggmarsh St. John, Ashenden Oakshott, and Bishop's Ickenham (all in *Uncle Dynamite*); Lower Shagley, East Wobsley, Ippleton, Pendlebury Parva, Little-Wigmarsh-in-the-Dell, Higgleford-cum-Wortlebury-beneath-the-Hill, Blotsam Regis, and Lower Smattering-on-the-Wissel (in the Mulliner tales), and the recurrent London suburb of Bottleton East. Most of his invented place-names are simply ridiculous in themselves, but sometimes they have implications for the story in which they occur, e.g. Matcham Scratchings as a country-house whose owners have a host of pet animals ("Good-Bye to all Cats"), or the home of a huntin' and shootin' family at Bludleigh Court ("Unpleasantness at Bludleigh Court").

Our risibilities are aroused by the names of many of Wodehouse's imaginary firms, especially publishers like Popgood and Grooly (*Uncle Dynamite, Cocktail Time,* etc.), Prodder and Wiggs ("Honeysuckle Cottage"), or Ye Panache Presse (*Uncle Dynamite*). Some of the names for lawyers' and tailors' firms make fun of the British habit of repeating the same name, as in Dykes, Dykes, and Pinweed, bespoke tailors (*Big Money*); the solicitors Shoesmith, Shoesmith, Shoesmith, and Shoesmith (*Money in the Bank*; *Ice in the Bedroom*); or the lawyers Messrs Peabody, Thrupp, Thrupp, Thrupp, and Peabody ("The Ordeal of Osbert Mulliner"). His Hollywood movie-forms have completely zany names, in keeping with the general atmostphere of what he has called "Dottyville-on-the-Pacific," as in the Superba-Llewellyn, the Perfecto-Zizzbaum, and the wholly fanciful Medulla-Oblongata-Glutz.

Patent medicines and other products also have comical names, such as Slimmo, "the sovereign remedy for obesity," which plays an important role in *Pigs Have Wings*; the dog-biscuits marketed by Freddie Threepwood's father-in-law's firm under the title of Donaldson's Dog-Joy, in competition with the equally alliterative Peterson's Pup-Food ("The Go-Getter") and with Todd's Tail-Wagger's Tid-Bits (*Full Moon*). Remedies for nervous and other ailments include Sugg's Soothine and Doctor Smythe's Tonic Swamp-Juice (mentioned several times by Uncle Fred). Most of Wodehouse's readers have often wished they could have a good dose of Mulliner's Buck-U-Uppo. Among makes of automobiles, the Buffy-Porson occurs frequently, as does also that engineering curiosity, the Widgeon Seven. In imitation of the names of swords like Excalibur and Durendal, Lord Ickenham has his great bath-sponge Joyeuse (*Uncle Fred in the Springtime*). Among imaginary books are such detective-stories as *Strychnine in the Soup*, *Blood on the Banisters* (in "Strychnine in the Soup"), *Excuse My Gat* (*Jeeves in the Offing*) and *The Mystery of the Pink Crayfish* (*Jeeves and the Feudal Spirit*). Lord Emsworth's favorite reading, in his pig-fancier-phase, is "Whiffle on *the Care of the Pig*".[15] Restaurants and night-clubs often have such names as The Feverish Cheese, The Startled Shrimp, The Mottled Oyster (*Jeeves and the Feudal Spirit*); The

Puce Ptarmigan ("The Story of Webster"); or The
Crushed Pansy, "the restaurant with a soul" (*Service
with a Smile*, ch. 8.2).

6.4. STYLISTIC DEVICES ON THE DISCOURSE-LEVEL

On the level of discourse,[19] stylistic devices are
generally of the type called rhetorical, i.e. involving the
skillful collocation of elements longer than the single
word (i.e. of phrases or sentences) to produce a given effect. In humor, the juxtaposition of elements may involve incongruity between the situations evoked or referred to, either directly in narration or in the author's
imagery (in similes, metaphors, and the like); or it may
involve citation of well-known phrases, either in their
original form or varied to suit the writer's purpose.

In their simplest form, Wodehouse's rhetorical devices
involve semantic incongruity, brought about through
the use of a given term or the evocation of a particular
situation, and then its immediate contradiction (total
or partial):

> From the penny-in-the-slot machine at the far
> end to the shed where the porter kept his brooms
> and buckets the platform was dark with what
> practically amounted to a sea of humanity. At least
> forty persons must have been present.
> —*Uncle Dynamite*, ch. 1
> His [Chimp Twist's] mood, in short, was one of
> saccharine benevolence. He was in the frame of
> mind when he would have patted a small boy on the
> head and given him sixpence, though it is probable
> that a moment later he would have tossed him for
> it and won it back again.
> —*Money in the Bank*, ch. 15
> Twice during these remarks, as the perfidy of
> Frederick Widgeon was made clearer and clearer to
> her, Sally had gasped—the first time like a Peking-
> ese choking on a bone of a size more suitable
> to a bloodhound, the second time like another

Pekingese choking on another bone of similar dimensions.

—*Ice in the Bedroom*, ch. 7

The incongruity may extend to the relation between the situations themselves as they follow each other in the story, either singly (as when Elizabeth Boyd is discomfited, in *Uneasy Money* [ch. 9], by Lord Dawlish's proving to be extremely skillful at handling bees when she had hoped he would be frightened away), or in sequence. One of the most amusing examples of the latter is the series of mishaps that befall Gussie Fink-Nottle, when he starts out for a fancy-dress-ball garbed as Mephistopheles, but gives the taxi-driver the wrong address, finds that he has left his money at home, returns there and finds that he has left his latch-key and admission-ticket in the house. It is locked because he has given the care-taker a holiday. He has a scuffle with the taxi-driver and frightens the latter away when Gussie's red devil's costume is revealed. He spends the rest of the night "ducking down side streets, skulking in alleyways, diving into dust bins" (*Right Ho, Jeeves*, ch. 5).

Allied to this is the SD of the enumeration, often with a carefully planned anticlimax at the end:

"She came down to school one Saturday and stood us school-boys a feed. Coffee, doughnuts, raspberry vinegar, two kinds of jam, two kinds of cake, ice cream, and sausages and mashed potatoes," said Berry, in whose memory the episode had never ceased to be green.

—*Big Money*, ch. 1

[Of the village hall at King's Deverill:] Its interior, like those of all the joints of its kind I've ever come across, was dingy and fuggy and smelled in about equal proportions of apples, chalk, damp plaster, Boy Scouts, and the sturdy English peasantry.

—*The Mating Season*, ch. 22

"The gentleman's already got a smoking-cap, poker chips, polo-sticks, a fishing-rod, a con-certina, a ukulele, a bowl of goldfish, a cocked hat and a sewing-machine," said Isadore.
"Ah?" said Bashford Braddock. "Then all he will require now is a sun helmet, a pair of puttees, and a pot of ointment for relieving alligator-bites."

—"The Ordeal of Osbert Mulliner"

"R!" said the second burglar, helping himself to more champagne and mixing in a little port, sherry, Italian vermouth, old brandy, and green Chartreuse to give it body.

—*ibid.*

Now slept the crimson petal and the white, and in the silent garden of Ashendon Manor nothing stirred save shy creatures of the night such as owls, mice, rats, gnats, bats and Constable Potter.

—*Uncle Dynamite*, ch. 6

In one instance, the important item is hidden in the middle of a similar long enumeration, which is then repeated without the item in question:

So saying, he produced from his trousers pocket a pencil, a ball of string, a piece of india rubber, threepence in bronze, the necklace, a packet of chewing gum, two buttons, and a small cough lozenge, and placed them on the table. He picked up the pencil, the ball of string, the piece of India rubber, the threepence, the chewing gum, the but-tons, and the lozenge, and returned them to his store.

—*The Luck of the Bodkins*, ch. 28

Best known of Wodehouse's SD's, however, is his imagery, involving similes, metaphors, and other types of comparison. The chief characteristic of his imagery is the wide range from which he draws his comparisons, using them in every instance to emphasize resem-blances which at first glance seem highly incongruous (and hence provoke the reader's laughter), but which at the same time are highly appropriate to the particular person or situation described. His imagery—carefully planned, of course, like all the rest of his writing—is therefore particularly vivid and apposite. Certain of his similes recur frequently, e.g. *He made a noise like a dying duck*[17] *in a thunderstorm,* or *The baby looked like a homicidal fried egg.* Other images occur only once, and it is hard to choose among them for exemplification. Every reader has his favorites; among mine are:

Even though this girl's slumber was not, as the poet Milton so beautifully puts it, "airy light," but rather reminiscent of a lumber-camp when the wood-sawing is proceeding at its briskest, he loved her still.
—"The Reverent Wooing of Archibald"
Talking to Elizabeth Bottsworth had always been like bellowing down a well in the hope of attracting the attention of one of the lesser infusoria at the bottom.
—"The Amazing Hat Mystery"
A sticky moisture had begun to bedew his brow, as if he had entered the hot room of some Turkish bath of the soul.
—*Uncle Dynamite,* ch. 3
The girl was like a chunk of ice-cream with spikes all over it.
—"Good-Bye to All Cats"
A sound like two or three pigs feeding rather noisily in the middle of a thunderstorm interrupted his meditation.
—*Leave It to Psmith,* ch. 7.1
That "ha, ha," so like the expiring quack of a duck dying of a broken heart.
—*The Mating Season,* ch. 12
"His I. Q. is about thirty points lower than that of a not too agile-minded jelly fish."
—*Full Moon,* ch. 6.6
"We are the parfait gentle knights, and we feel that it ill beseems us to make a beeline for a girl like a man charging into a railway restaurant for a bowl of soup."
—*Thank You, Jeeves,* ch. 4

The light faded from her face, and in its stead
there appeared the hurt, bewildered look of a bare-
foot dancer who, while halfway through the Vision
of Salome, steps on a tin tack.
                                        —*ibid.*, ch. 9
"Have you ever heard Sir Watkyn Bassett dealing with a bowl of soup? It's not unlike the Scot-
tish express going through a tunnel."
                          —*The Code of the Woosters*, ch. 4
There was a snake in his Garden of Eden, a
crumpled leaf in his bed of roses, a grain of sand
in his spiritual spinach.
                               —*Pigs Have Wings*, ch. 1
I received the impression of a sort of blend of
Tallulah Bankhead and a policewoman.
                                   —"Noblesse Oblige"
He was in the overwrought state when a fly
treading a little too heavily on the carpet is
enough to make a man think he's one of the ex-
tras in *All Quiet On The Western Front*.
                          —"The Luck of the Stiffhams"

Such a list could be continued almost indefinitely; a
whole volume could be compiled simply by excerpting
all the imagery which Wodehouse uses in his stories.

If such a volume were put together, its contents
would have to be arranged in some way, probably
according to the semantic sources of the images involved. It would, I believe, be found that Wodehouse
jaws on almost all the phenomena known—at first
hand or through extensive reading—to a well-educated
member of the modern English-speaking world. He has
images drawn from the physical world (animal,
vegetable, and mineral), as known to us through our
five senses and through scientific investigation; from our
culture's philosophy and religion; from the myths,
legends, and literature of our own and other cultures;
and from the manifold activities of humans in all their
different pursuits. What has been said of the street-
names of Rome could also be said of Wodehouse's
images: a complete understanding of all their references

would lead one to an extensive and thorough ac-
quaintance with most of what is important in our
history and culture.

Certain semantic sources are particularly prominent
in Wodehouse's imagery, however: the animal world,
sports (especially golf), and the world of the theatre
and musical comedy. (This is probably not fortuitous,
in view of his interest in these three fields.)[18] Opening
one of his books (*Blandings Castle*) at random, at one
of the pages of "Company for Gertrude," in three pages
I find such gems as these:

> They proceeded down to dinner in a perfect gale
> of merriment, rather like a chorus of revellers
> exiting after a concerted number in an old-fash-
> ioned comic opera.
> True, he [Lord Emsworth] had taken into his
> home what appeared to be a half-witted acrobat.
> "Medicine is to the guv'nor what catnip is to
> the cat."

In this respect, too, Bertie Wooster seems to be, as has
been suggested,[19] somewhat of a projection of Wodehouse himself: Bertie is fond of animals, especially
cats; he goes in for golf and swimming; and he shows
himself, at various points, quite familiar with the musical theatre.[20] Bertie, too, draws much of his imagery
from these sources, as when he speaks (*Stiff Upper Lip,
Jeeves*, ch. 14, 15) of:

> [. . .] Spode, who had at that moment en-
> tered left center.
> "I hate you, I hate you!" cried Madeline, a thing
> I didn't know anyone ever said except in the second
> act of a musical comedy.

Horse-racing, also, is a common source of imagery, as
in Bertie's description of how his Aunt Dahlia, the butler Seppings, and he hasten to the chef Anatole's room
(*Right Ho, Jeeves*, ch. 20), a parody of race-reporting:

[. . .] I put down my plate and hastened after her, Seppings following at a loping gallop.

[. . .] At the top of the first flight she must have led by a matter of half a dozen lengths, and was still shaking off my challenge when she rounded into the second. At the next landing, however, the grueling going appeared to tell on her, for she slackened off a little and showed symptoms of roaring, and by the time we were in the straight we were running practically neck and neck. Our entry into Anatole's room was as close a finish as you could have wished to see.

Result:
1. Aunt Dahlia.
2. Bertram.
3. Seppings.

Won by a short head. Half a staircase separated second and third.

6.5 QUOTATION AND VARIATION

Every reader of Wodehouse is immediately struck by the extent to which his stories abound in quotations from classical and other authors, deftly adapted to his purpose of the moment.[21] Like his similes, Wodehouse's quotations come from extremely varied sources, attesting to wide reading on his part—begun, doubtless, in his school-years, and kept up ever since. Among his sources, the Bible and Shakespeare are especially frequently quoted. Bertie Wooster, in many of the stories about him, makes it clear that he was a Scripture-knowledge-shark at school (and once won a prize therefor). He is constantly referring to such Biblical characters as Balaam's ass, King Belshazzar, and Jael the wife of Heber. Most of the time he quotes the Bible accurately, but sometimes he distorts the quotation, as when (*Thank You, Jeeves*, ch. 20) he refers to

[. . .] a chap who, as the Bible puts it, if you say Go, he cometh, and if you say Come, he goeth [. . .].

Other Wodehouse characters also quote or misquote the Bible and Shakespeare from time to time:

> "Pongo", said Lord Ickenham, "is is terrific form. He bestrides the world like a Colossus. It would not be too much to say that Moab is his washpot and over what's-its-name has he cast his shoe." [22]
> —*Uncle Dynamite*, ch. 5

In many instances, as in the ones just cited, Wodehouse varies his source to make it fit the context. In *The Girl on the Boat* (ch. 17.2), he reverses the relationship between Othello and Desdemona, to describe the love of the timid Eustace Hignett for the elephant-huntress Jane Hubbard:

> For three days Jane Hubbard had been weaving her spell about Eustace Hignett, and now she monopolised his entire horizon. She had spoken, like Othello, of antres vast and deserts idle, rough quarries, rocks and hills whose heads touched heaven, and of the cannibals that each other eat, the Anthropophagi, and men whose heads do grow beneath their shoulders. This to hear would Eustace Hignett seriously incline, and swore, i' faith, 'twas strange, 'twas passing strange, 'twas pitiful, 'twas wondrous pitiful. He loved her for the dangers she had passed, and she loved him that he did pity them. In fact, one would have said that it was all over except buying the licence, had it not been for the fact that his very admiration served to keep Eustace from pouring out his heart. It seemed incredible to him that the queen of her sex, a girl who had chatted on terms of equality with African head-hunters and who swatted alligators as though they were flies, could ever lower herself to care for a man who looked like the "after-taking" advertisement of a patent food.

in *Uncle Dynamite* (ch. 6.2), Lord Ickenham greets Bill Oakshott with "Well met by moonlight, proud Oakshott."

In other passages, Wodehouse gives the quoted passage directly as in the original, without change in the citation itself, but often with something added in the context to make it ridiculously apposite:

> One of the reasons why he preferred not to see much of Stanhope Twine was that the latter, when he felt strongly on any subject, was inclined to squeak and gibber like the sheeted dead in the Roman streets a little ere the mightiest Julius' fell.
> —*Something Fishy*, ch. 9

[Baxter to Psmith on the terrace of Blandings Castle:] "Oh, it's you?" he said morosely.

"I in person," said Psmith genially. "Awake, beloved! Awake, for morning in the bowl of night has flung the stone that puts the stars to flight; and lo! the hunter of the East has caught the Sultan's turret in the noose of light. The Sultan himself," he added, "you will find behind yonder window, speculating idly on your motives for bunging flower-pots at him."
> —*Leave It to Psmith*, ch. 11.5

> The thoughts of youth, said Henry Wadsworth Longfellow (1805-1882), are long long thoughts, and so, when the conditions are right, are those of middle age.
> —*A Pelican at Blandings*, ch. 10.3

> Julius Caesar, who liked to have men—and presumably pigs—around him that were fat, would have welcomed her without hesitation to his personal entourage.
> —*ibid.*, ch. 7.2

> "Others abide our question. Thou art free," was the verdict of London's gilded youth on Archibald Mulliner when considered purely in the light of a man who could imitate a hen laying an egg.
> —"The Reverent Wooing of Archibald"

> However much an Aberdeen terrier may bear 'mid snow and ice a banner with the strange device Excelsior, he nearly always has to be content with dirty looks and the sharp, passionate bark.
> —*Stiff Upper Lip, Jeeves*, ch. 8

In addition to quotations, varied and unvaried, Wodehouse's stories are full of clichés, particularly from
bilge-literature, detective-stories, and adventure-stories.
These, too, he uses either out of place or varied for humorous effect:

> Sometimes in our wanderings about the world we
> meet men of whom it is said that they have passed
> through the furnace. Of Sir Aylmer it would be
> more correct to say that he had passed through the
> frigidaire.
> —*Uncle Dynamite*, ch. 6
> Presently from behind us there sounded in the
> night the splintering crash of a well-kicked plate of
> sandwiches, accompanied by the muffled oaths of a
> strong man in his wrath.
> —*Right Ho, Jeeves*, ch. 15
> He was an optimist and throughout his check-
> ered career had always clung stoutly to the view that
> no matter how darkly the clouds might lower the
> sun would eventually come shining through, but
> this time it looked as if the sun had other intentions.
> —*A Pelican at Blandings*, ch. 4.3
> George Cyril might rather closely resemble some-
> one for whom the police were spreading a dragnet
> in the expectation of making an arrest shortly, but
> nobody could deny his great gifts. He knew his pigs.
> —*Service with a Smile*, sh. 1

> [In a Hollywood studio] The world seems very
> far away: Outside, the sun beats down on the con-
> crete, and occasionally you will see a man in shirt
> sleeves driving a truck to a distant set, while ever
> and anon the stillness is broken by the shrill cry of
> some wheeling supervisor. But for the most part
> a forlorn silence prevails.
> —*"The Castaways"*

These, then, are some samples of Wodehouse's SD's,
classified and arranged roughly according to their nature and sources. However, it is not enough to enumer-

ate them and put them into pigeon-holes; we must see what Wodehouse does with them when he brings them together into a unified stylistic whole. We shall examine this aspect of his writing in the following chapter.

Notes to Chapter 6

1. Here and in following quotations, stylistic devices will be given in SMALL CAPITALS, and the stylistic context, if any, in which they are set will be in *italics*.

2. Different speech-communities, or different groups in any given speech-community, often have varying reactions to such jarring elements. Modern Italians' sense of *concinnitas*, "appropriateness of usage," makes them object to the mingling of colloquialisms with scientific discourse in, say, the Italian translation of Hockett 1968; and even I, a notorious "liberal" in linguistic matters, am not pleased when I read, at the end of a supposedly scientific article, discussing the concept of the phoneme, the sentences "As generativists, if we acknowledged him [the phoneme], then it was as an illegitimate child. Perhaps we can now recognize the little bastard for what he really is" (Schane 1971:520).

3. Most theoreticians of humor recognize incongruity as an essential factor, e.g. Eastman 1936:51; Tidwell (ed.) 1956:522-523, Fernández de la Vega 1963; Fry 1963.

4. Cf. the observations of Hockett (1958:308) on this particular formation, whose particular force is due to the relative infrequency of normal words in *-wards*. Nonce-formations with this suffix are, however, perhaps more frequent in British than in American English; the detective-story-writer R. Austin Freeman, in one of his stories (*Mr. Pottermack's Oversight*, ch. 7), has Dr. Thorndyke walk *Templewards*.

5. In Hall 1973.

6. This way of talking was popular with certain amiable but affected young men in the first decade or so of the twentieth century in England, known as Nuts or Knuts (cf. Usborne 1961:69-70).

7. This rhetorical device is akin to the Old Germanic kenning (e.g. saying *the ship of the desert* for 'camel'), or, more precisely, to what Snorri Sturluson termed the *ofljóst*.

8. For a complete listing of the names of the characters, places, and things in Wodehouse's stories up to 1969, cf. the lists in Jasen 1971:263-290.

9. Note that *Bashford*, for instance, is a real name: there is, at the American Museum of Natural History, the on-going project of the Bashford Dean Bibliography of Fishes. Wodehouse is of course playing on the British meaning of *bash* 'strike violently, smash with a blow'.

10. A *dibble* is a hole in the ground, here clearly suggesting the holes of a golf-course.

11. For the theory of secondary associations, cf. Hockett 1958:296-298.

12. This nickname is identical with the British colloquial adjective

barmy 'crazy', a re-spelling of *balmy* (with semantic development through 'happy' to "silly'.

13. In the American edition of this story (*The Return of Jeeves*), this name was changed to Towcester (= *toaster*).

14. *Bring On the Girls*, ch. 11.

15. Everywhere except in *Galahad at Blandings* (1965), the author of this *Jeeves da cheuet* of Lord Emsworth's is *Whiffle*; but in that one book, he is introduced as a live character, and is redemptioned *Augustus Whipple* (presumably because someone—Wodehouse himself or some editor—thought the earlier name too unlikely or in some other way unacceptable). Similarly, for some unknown reason, Jeeves' temporary substitute, one Brinkley (in *Thank You, Jeeves*), when he reappears in *Much Obliged, Jeeves*, is named Bingley.

16. For discourse-analysis in general, cf. especially Grimes 1972.

17. Apparently *a dying duck* or *a dying rooster* was some kind of inflatable rubber toy which made a peculiar noise as the air slowly oozed out of it. In *Uneasy Money* (ch. 1), Lord Dawlish is accosted in Shaftesbury Avenue by "a vagrant of almost the maximum seediness, from whose midriff there protruded a trayful of a strange welter of collar-studs, shoe-laces, rubber rings, buttonhooks, and dying roosters," one of which the panhandler inflates and permits to die noisily. Even without this knowledge, however, the ordinary reader can be amused by the comparison of a noise with that of a live duck *in extremis* drowned out by a thunderstorm.

18. As shown in his autobiographical works *Performing Flea* and *Over Seventy*, and commented on by all his critics.

19. Cf. Usborne 1961:162-165.

20. He has an actress friend, Marion Wardour (whose name is taken from Wardour-street in London, in the heart of the theatrical district); he mentions various bits of popular music from time to time; and in *The Mating Season* (ch. 6), he shows himself a skillful improviser of highly Wodehousian verses for a song.

21. Cf. Usborne 1961:73-76; Olney 1962; French 1966:103-105; Voorhees 1966:162-167.

22. The original quotation is "Moab is my washpot; over Edom will I cast out my show" (Psalm 60.8, in the King James version).

7

Incongruity and Stylistic Rhythm

In his use of virtually all the resources of both formal and informal English, Wodehouse does not overwork any single stylistic device at any particular point. Rather, he spreads his use of all possible variations thin enough so that they do not become tiresome, introducing each one at just the right place on every occasion. Usborne (1961:159-161), in his analysis of a passage of Bertie Wooster's narrative, points out the numerous elements which render it effectively humorous, mostly in terms of the sources involved, and refers to "the highly disciplined and tightly controlled Wodehouse burble." This description might well be applied to all of Wodehouse's use of English, in its structural as well as its semantic aspects.

As the reader progresses from one word, one sentence, one paragraph to the next, there can be a variation in the rate at which SD's are introduced, either by a change of functional level and variety, or in the semantics of the passage involved. The variation in rate of change thus introduced is somewhat analogous to that in the harmonic structure of a musical composition—i.e. whether the changes of key are few and come only infrequently (as in most seventeenth- and eighteenth-century music), or whether they are many and occur in rapid succession (as is increasingly the case in the nineteenth and early wentieth centuries). The rate of key-change in a composition is often termed *harmonic* rhythm, which may

117

vary from slow to fast. Similarly, we may speak, in discussing the rate of occurrence of SD's and SC's in a literary work, of its *stylistic rhythm*. In serious literature, particularly tragedy and epic, loftiness of style is maintained by keeping the stylistic rhythm slow, fitting SD's cunningly into their SC, and differentiating this latter only gradually and subtly.[1] In humor, on the other hand, the stylistic rhythm is much more rapid, and the more discrepancy there is between the SD's and their SC and SB, the greater is the humor. Even here, however, there is room for considerable subtlety in the way in which a writer, by skillful use of his SD's, tickles our risibilities.

This can be seen in the opening passage of *The Luck of the Bodkins*, which is justly famous as one of the most effective of all of Wodehouse's beginnings. Let us look at the first 301 words. (I have put the SD's, i.e. the places which make me smile or laugh, in small capitals; and their SC, if any, leading up to them, in italics. Every tenth word is followed by its decile-number to enable the reader to make easy reference when he comes to the discussion following the text.)

Into the face of the young man who sat on (10) the terrace of the Hotel Magnifique at Cannes there had (20) crept a look of furtive shame, the shifty, hangdog look (30) WHICH ANNOUNCES THAT AN ENGLISHMAN IS ABOUT TO TALK FRENCH(40). One of the things that Gertrude Butterwick had impressed upon (50) Monty Bodkin when he left for his holiday on the (60) Riviera was that he must be sure to practise his (70) French, and Gertrude's word was law. So now, though he (80) knew it was going to MAKE HIS NOSE TICKLE (90), he said:

"ER, GARÇON."
"*M'sieur?*"
"ER, *garçon*, ESKER *vous avez* (100) *un* SPOT *de* L'*encre et une* PIECE *de papier* (110)—NOTE-PAPIER, *vous savez—et une enveloppe et une plume?*" (120)
"*Bien, m'sieur.*"

THE STRAIN WAS TOO GREAT. Monty RELAPSED into (130) his native tongue.
"I want to write a letter," he (140) said. And having, like all lovers, *rather a tendency to* (150) *share his romance with the world,* he would probably have (160) added "TO THE SWEETEST GIRL ON EARTH," had not (170) the waiter already *bounded off* LIKE A RETRIEVER, to return (180) a few minutes later with the FIXINGS.
"*V'la* SIR! ZERE (190) you are sir," said the waiter. He was engaged to (200) a girl in Paris who had told him that when (210) on the Riviera he must be sure to practise his (220) English. "EENK—PIN—PIPPER—*and a* LIDDLE *bit of* BLODDIN-PIPPER" (230).
"*Oh,* MERCI," said Monty, well pleased at this efficiency, "*Thanks.* (240) *Right-ho.*"
"*Right-ho,* M'SIEUR," said the waiter.
Left alone (250), Monty lost no time in spreading paper on the table (260), taking up the pen and dipping it in the ink. (270) SO FAR, SO GOOD. But now, as so often happened (280) when he started to write to the girl he loved (290), there occurred a STAGE WAIT. He paused, WONDERING HOW TO (300) begin. (130)

Now let us look at the numerical ratio between the SB, SC's, and SD's in these 301 words, and examine the nature and function of the various parts of the passage:

Words	Number of words	Nature	Function
1-27	27	SB	Narration: sets scene
28-30	3	SC	Variation to informal standard (slightly colloquial *shifty, hangdog,* modifying *look*), preparing for SD
31-40	10	SD	Semantically incongruous remark set in formal standard (esp. *announces*)
41-86	46	SB	Further back-ground and previous history; slightly trite terminology, as in bilge-novels (e.g. *Gertrude's word was law*)

87-90	4	SD	Semantically incongruous element, slightly informal construction and lexical level
91-92	2	SB	Narration
93-94	2	SD	Incongruous combination of English informal interjection *er* and French (English accent in French not indicated in spelling)
95	1	SC	French
96	1	SD	English interjection in midst of French
99-101	3	SC	French
102	1	SD	English word (informal, Briticism) in French
103	1	SC	French
104	1	SD	Faulty French construction (*de l'encre* instead of *d'encre*)
105-107	3	SC	French
108	1	SD	Anglicism in French (use of false cognate)
109-110	2	SC	French
111-112	2	SD	English-style compound in French; use of false cognate
113-122	10	SC	French
123-127	5	SD	Trite observation in style of bilge-literature; semantic incongruity
128	1	SB	Proper name, subject of sentence
129	1	SD	Use of over-technical term (quasi-medical)
130-146	17	SB	Narration
147-156	10	SC	Semantic incongruity; sets stage for 162-167; use of informal *rather*
157-161	5	SB	Narration
162-167	5	SC	Semantic incongruity (exaggeration)
168-173	6	SB	Narration; return to formal standard marked by inversion of verb and subject
174-175	2	SC	Use of unexpectedly literal verb *bounded off*; prepares for SD of 176-178
176-178	3	SD	Comparison with eager dog
179-186	8	SB	Narration
187	1	SD	Shift of level to informal standard (very colloquial)
188	1	SC	French (used by Frenchman)
189	1	SD	English in same utterance, used by Frenchman
190	1	SD	Frenchman's pronunciation of English

191-192	2	SC	Frenchman's use of English colloquial word-order
193-221	19	SB	Narration; slight semantic incongruity in parallel of waiter's situation with Monty's
222-224	3	SD	Frenchman's pronunciation of English
225-226	2	SC	Normal English (at least in orthography)
227	1	SD	Frenchman's pronunciation of English
228-229	2	SC	Normal English (note absence of possible *beet* for *bit*)
230	1	SD	Frenchman's pronunciation of English
231	1	SC	Informal standard English interjection
232	1	SD	Use of French word after English interjection, by speaker of English
233-238	6	SB	Narration (note use of adjective-phrase following noun, rather formal)
239-242	4	SC	Shift to informal standard conversational interjection
243-245	3	SD	Frenchman's echoing of English interjection and shift to French immediately thereafter
246-270	25	SB	Narration; slight semantic incongruity between detailed enumeration of events and their insignificance
271-274	4	SD	Shift to informal standard colloquial and unexpected semantic content in midst of formal narration
275-293	19	SB	Narration
294-295	2	SD	Semantic incongruity in metaphor, emphasized by use of technical term from theatrical usage
296-297	2	SB	Narration
298-301	4	SD	Semantic incongruity (delay in action after build-up)

It is worth noting that whereas the narrative portions of this passage involve 186 words, or approximately 62 per cent of the total number, a considerably greater percentage, be it noted, than the over-all average mentioned in § 4.1, no single stretch of narrative is longer than 46 words, and the five other major narrative stretches are only 27, 16, 19, 25, and 19 words respectively. The six sentences, taken together, show an average of 25.3 words apiece. This is very close to the average to be obtained in Wodehouse's mature narrative prose in general: in the passages from *Full Moon* analyzed previously (§ 5.3) for the number of syllables, per word, the over-all sentence-length, in comparison with Mark Twain and Henry James, is as follows:

	Words per sentence
Wodehouse (narrative)	26.4
Wodehouse (dialogue)	8.2
Twain	19.2
James	35.5

Wodehouse keeps his narrative constantly broken up by SD's in many instances embedded in a preparatory SC, but in other cases not. Both SD's and SC's involve short passages, never more than ten words at the most. They follow each other at very short intervals, thereby producing the well-known "rapid-fire" effect of Wodehousian simile, metaphor, and "cross-talk" dialogue. In his earlier stories, as we have seen (in § 4.1), the amount of narrative can be considerably greater in proportion to the dialogue. It is rare, however, even in such relatively serious earlier stories as *The Little Nugget* or *The Coming of Bill*, that an expository passage does not contain some at least mildly incongruous SD, reminding the reader that this story is, after all, by P. G. Wodehouse (and not, say, George Gissing or Thomas Hardy).

To obtain a sample of the proportion of conversation to narration, in a typical expository (rather than introductory) chapter, let us turn to chapter 11 of *The Luck of the Bodkins*. In the first chapter, we have been introduced to Monty Bodkin and his absent fiancee Gertrude Butterwick (from whom he receives a curt notification, at the end of the chapter, that their engagement is broken off), the movie-magnate Ivor Llewellyn, and his sister-in-law Mabel Spence, at Cannes. For the second chapter, the scene shifts to Waterloo Station in London (in the

American version, the docks at Southampton), where a number of further characters are introduced and the action is carried forward, especially as concerns the relationship between Gertrude and Monty. The entire chapter contains 2599 words, of which 1430 are narration (55%) and 1169 dialogue (45%). The longest stretch of narration is at the outset, 379 words, interrupted by only three words of dialogue after 223 words, and then by another fifteen of dialogue after a further 106 of narration. Thereafter, there are only five stretches of exposition of over fifty words, containing 64, 89, 181, 93, and 280 words respectively. In every longer narrative stretch there are one or more humorous SD's, often incongruities pointed out by Wodehouse in his capacity of story-teller. Thus, in the long stretch of narration at the beginning of the chapter, there are such remarks as:

> Ivor Llewellyn was there, talking to the reporters about IDEALS AND THE FUTURE OF THE SCREEN. [...] Ambrose Tennyson, the novelist, was there, asking the bookstall clerk if he had anything BY AMBROSE TENNYSON.[. . .]*The scene, in short, presented* A GAY AND ANIMATED APPEARANCE.
>
> In this, IT DIFFERED SUBSTANTIALLY from the young man *with the dark circles under his eyes* who was PROPPING HIMSELF UP against a penny-in-the-slot machine. An undertaker, passing at that moment, *would have looked at this young man* SHARPLY, SCENTING BUSINESS. *So would a* BUZZARD.

By far the greater part of the dialogue in this chapter consists of animated give-and-take, with only four speeches containing over fifty words (87, 60, 146, and 185, respectively) in the course of the chapter. Of the conversations, eleven contain four or more speeches, most of them very short (twelve to fifteen words at the most, with only a few exceptions). The following stretches of dialogue, between Ambrose Tennyson's brother Reggie and his cousin Gertrude Butterwick, are typical:

"Well, it's about time [you went to Canada, says Gertrude]. *Work is what you want."*
"WORK IS NOT WHAT I WANT. I HATE THE THOUGHT OF IT."
"You needn't be so cross."
"YES, I NEED," said Reggie. "CROSSER, IF I COULD MANAGE IT. *Work is what I want,* FORSOOTH! *Of all the* SILLY, DRIVELLING, FATHEADED REMARKS . . . "
"Don't be so rude."
[. . .]
"I've been having—*well, I wouldn't attempt* TO PRONOUNCE THE WORD AT A MOMENT LIKE THIS, *but I dare say you know what I mean.* BEGINS WITH 'HAL'."
"Hallucinations?"
"That's right. SEEING CHAPS WHO AREN'T THERE."
"Don't DROOL, Reggie."
"I'M NOT DROOLING. Just now, I opened my eyes— WHY, ONE CANNOT SAY—and I saw my brother Ambrose."

Note, in this passage, the SD of having a character begin to say a long or otherwise high-falutin' word and then be unable to continue, depending on his interlocutor to supply the rest. This SD is especially frequent in Bertie Wooster's conversation or first-person narration (cf. § 6.3). Note also the use of the incongruously objective *one*, which here has a slight connotation of medical parlance.[2] In "The Man Who Gave Up Smoking", the continued use of *one* for 'I', 'me', and 'you', by the art-critic Cyprian Rossiter (echoed by Ignatius Mulliner, at first seriously and then ironically) conveys an over-tone of affected pseudo-artistic jargon.

Wodehouse's peculiar effectiveness as a comic writer, in contradistinction to that of many other humorists (e.g. Compton Mackenzie, Denis Mackail, Harry Leon Wilson, James Thurber), consists especially in his skillful alternation of a SB of narration in formal standard English with frequent SC's and SD's, of all types and semantic origins, with a rapid, kaleidoscopically varying stylistic rhythm. To analyse the entire corpus of Wodehouse's writings in this way would, using non-mechanised techniques of study, take easily one, perhaps more, life-times of work, and probably more man-hours than he himself has put into producing it. I believe, nevertheless, that such a total study would con-firm the basic findings of this investigation.

In concluding, it may be well to compare Wodehouse's style with that of a writer who, at first glance, may seem quite dissimilar—Dante Alighieri (1265-1321), in his *Divine Comedy*. Their aims are of course dissimilar: Dante's, to save the human soul; Wodehouse's, to amuse it while it is waiting to be saved. Yet there is more similarity, in subject-matter and in style, than might perhaps be thought. Both give, in their semantics, an over-all, nearly encyclopaedic view of the world of their times and its inherited culture. Each has, in his style, a rich SB, with a great plenitude and diversity of effec-tive SD's, set in carefully prepared SC's. They both ob-tain their effects by complete mastery over their media— Italian verse on the one hand, English prose on the other. Each, in his own way, has shown himself worthy of the epithet Dante applies to the Provencal trouba-dour Arnaut Daniel, *il miglior fabbro del parlar materno*.

Notes to Chapter 7

1. So much so, on occasion, as to have justified Sainte-Beuve's famous remark about Racine: "Il rase la prose, mais avec des ailes."
2. For discussion of a similar use of the definite article by Bertie Wooster, cf. Usborne 1961:160-161.

Lists of Novels and Short Stories

These two alphabetical lists are intended to facilitate the reader's dating of the novels and short stories referred to in the text. In the list of novels, the titles given them in England are listed alphabetically, with the American title (if different) in the middle column, and the year of their publication in book-form on the right. In the list of short stories, the middle column gives the collection in which they were published, and the right-hand column the date of its publication. For a complete listing of all of Wodehouse's prose publications, cf. Jasen 1970.

1. BOOKS

English Title	American Title (if different)	Date
Barmy in Wonderland	Angel Cake	1952
Big Money		1931
Bill the Conqueror		1924
Blandings Castle		1935
Bring On the Girls		1953
Cocktail Time		1958
The Code of the Woosters		1938
The Coming of Bill	Their Mutual Child	1917
Company for Henry	The Purloined Paperweight	1967

The Crime Wave at Blandings		1937
A Damsel in Distress		1919
Do Butlers Burgle Banks?		1968
Doctor Sally	"The Medicine Girl"	1932
French Leave		1956
Frozen Assets	Biffen's Millions	1964
Full Moon		1947
Galahad at Blandings	The Brinkmanship of Galahad Threepwood	1965
A Gentleman of Leisure	The Intrusion of Jimmy	1910
The Girl in Blue		1970
The Girl on the Boat		1922
The Gold Bat		1904
Good Morning, Bill		1928
Heavy Weather		1933
Hot Water		1932
Ice in the Bedroom	The Ice in the Bedroom	1961
The Inimitable Jeeves	Jeeves	1923
Jeeves and the Feudal Spirit	Bertie Wooster Sees It Through	1954
Jeeves in the Offing	How Right You Are, Jeeves	1960
Jill the Reckless	The Little Warrior	1920
Joy in the Morning		1946
Laughing Gas		1936
Leave It to Psmith		1923
The Little Nugget		1913
Lord Emsworth and Others	The Crime Wave at Blandings	1937
Louder and Funnier		1932
Love Among the Chickens		1906
The Luck of the Bodkins		1936
The Man With Two Left Feet		1917
The Mating Season		1949
Meet Mr. Mulliner		1927
Mike		1909
Money for Nothing		1928
Money in the Bank		1942
Mr. Mulliner Speaking		1929
Much Obliged, Jeeves	Jeeves and the Tie That Binds	1971

Mulliner Nights		1933
My Man Jeeves		1919
Not George Washington		1907
Nothing Serious		1950
The Old Reliable		1951
Over Seventy	America, I like You	1957
Pearls, Girls, and M Bodkin		1972
A Pelican at Blandings	No Nudes Is Good Nudes	1969
Performing Flea	Author, Author!	1953
Pigs Have Wings		1952
The Pothunters		1902
A Prefect's Uncle		1903
The Prince and Betty		1912
Psmith in the City		1910
Psmith, Journalist		1915
Right Ho, Jeeves	Brinkley Manor	1934
Ring for Jeeves	The Return of Jeeves	1953
Sam the Sudden	Sam in the Suburbs	1925
Service with a Smile		1961
The Small Bachelor		1927
Something Fishy	The Butler Did It	1957
Something Fresh	Something New	1915
Spring Fever		1948
Stiff Upper Lip, Jeeves		1963
Summer Lightning	Fish Preferred	1929
Summer Moonshine		1937
The Swoop!		1909
Tales of St. Austin's		1903
Thank You, Jeeves		1934
Uncle Dynamite		1948
Uncle Fred in the Springtime		1939
Uneasy Money		1916
Very Good, Jeeves		1930
William Tell Told Again		1904
Young Men In Spats		1936

2. Short Stories

Title	Collection	Date
The Amazing Hat Mystery	Young Men in Spats	1936
Archibald and the Masses	Young Men in Spats	1936
The Artistic Career of Corky	My Man Jeeves	1919
Aunt Agatha Speaks Her Mind	The Inimitable Jeeves	1923
Bertie Changes His Mind	Carry On, Jeeves	1925
Best Seller	Mulliner Nights	1933
Birth of a Salesman	Nothing Serious	1950
The Bishop's Move	Meet Mr. Mulliner	1927
Butlers and the Buttled	Louder and Funnier	1932
The Castaways	Blandings Castle	1935
Cats Will Be Cats	Mulliner Nights	1933
The Clicking of Cuthbert	The Clicking of Cuthbert	1922
The Code of the Mulliners	Young Men In Spats	1936
Company for Gertrude	Blandings Castle	1935
The Crime Wave at Blandings	Lord Emsworth and Others	1937
Extricating Young Gussie	The Man With Two Left Feet	1917
The Go-Getter	Blandings Castle	1935
Good-Bye To All Cats	Young Men in Spats	1936
Honeysuckle Cottage	Meet Mr. Mulliner	1927
Jeeves and the Dog McIntosh	Very Good, Jeeves	1930
Jeeves and the Impending Doom	Very Good, Jeeves	1930
Jeeves and the Old School Chum	Very Good, Jeeves	1930
Jeeves and the Yuletide Spirit	Very Good, Jeeves	1930
Jeeves Exerts the Old Cerebellum	The Inimitable Jeeves	1923
The Knightly Quest of Mervyn	Mulliner Nights	1933
Lord Emsworth and the Girl Friend	Blandings Castle	1935
The Luck of the Stiffhams	Young Men in Spats	1936

Bibliography

Aldridge, John W. 1958. P.G. Wodehouse: the lesson of the young master. New World Writing, no. 13. New York: New American Library. Reprinted as Introduction to Selected Stories by P. G. Wodehouse xi-xxv (New York: Random House, 1958).

Bloomfield, Leonard: Language. New York: Holt.

Eastman, Max. 1936. Enjoyment of laughter. New York:Simon and Schuster.

Fernández de la Vega, Celestino. 1963. O segredo do humor. Vigo: Galaxia.

Fiedler, Leslie. 1960. Love and death in the American novel. New York: Criterion Books.

Flesch, Rudolf. 1949. The art of readable writing. New York: Harper.

French, R. B. D. 1966. P. G. Wodehouse. Edinburgh and London: Oliver and Boyd. (New York: Barnes and Noble, 1967.)

Fries, Charles C. 1940. American English grammar. New York: Appleton-Century.

Fry, William F., Jr. 1963. Sweet madness: a study of humor. Palo Alto, California: Pacific Books.

Gillen, Charles E. 1969. H. H. Munro (Saki). New York: Twayne Publishers.

Grimes, Joseph E. 1972. The thread of discourse [preliminary edition]. Ithaca, N.Y.: Cornell University, Division of Modern Languages.

Hall, Robert A., Jr. 1963. Cultural symbolism in literature.
Ithaca, N.Y.: Linguistica.
_____. 1964a. P. G. Wodehouse and the English language.
Annali della Scuola Orientale di Napoli—Sezione Germanica 7.103-121.
_____. 1964b. Introductory linguistics. Philadelphia: Chilton
Books.
_____. 1964c. To hyphenate or not to hyphenate. English
Journal 53.662-665.
_____. 1967. Antonio Fogazzaro e la crisi dell'Italia moderna.
Ithaca, N.Y.: Linguistica.
_____. 1969a. Incongruity and stylistic rhythm in P. G. Wode-
house. Annali della Scuola Orientale di Napoli—Sezione
Germanica 11.135-144.
_____. 1969b. Review of Y. Malkiel: Essays on linguistic
themes. General Linguistics 9.185-195.
_____. 1973. The transferred epithet in P. G. Wodehouse.
Linguistic Inquiry 4.92-94.
_____. Forthcoming-a. Primicias estilísticas de P. G. Wode-
house. To appear in a Festschrift.
_____. Forthcoming-b. The ending of P. G. Wodehouse's
Leave It to Psmith. To appear in *Notes and Queries.*
Hayward, John. 1941. P. G. Wodehouse. The Saturday Book.
London: Hutchinson.
Hockett, Charles F. 1958. A course in modern linguistics. New
York: Macmillan.
_____. 1968. The state of the art. The Hague: Mouton. Italian
translation: La linguistica americana contemporanea (Bari:
Laterza, 1970).
Ives, Sumner. 1950. A theory of literary dialect. Tulane Studies
in English 2.137-182.
Jaggard, Geoffrey. 1967. Wooster's world. London: MacDonald.
_____. 1968. Blandings the blest. London: MacDonald.
Jasen, David. 1970. A bibliography and reader's guide to the
first editions of P. G. Wodehouse. New Haven, Connecticut:
Archon Books.
_____. 1973. P. G. Wodehouse: the life of a master. London:
Garnstone Press.
Kenyon, John S. 1948. Cultural levels and functional varieties
of English. College English 10.31-36. Reprinted in Harold B.
Allen (ed.): Applied English Linguistics 215-221 (New York:

Appleton-Century-Crofts, 1958).

Lardner, John. 1948. Wodehouse past and present. The New Yorker, May 22, 1948, pp. 104-106.

Olney, Clarke. 1962. Wodehouse and the poets. The Georgia Review 16.392-399 (Winter, 1962).

Orwell, George. 1944/46. In defense of P. G. Wodehouse. The Windmill 1·2 10-18. Reprinted in Orwell: Dickens, Dali and others 222-243 (New York: Reynal and Hitchcock, 1946); also in The Collected Essays, Journalism, and Letters of George Orwell 3.341-355 (London: Secker and Warburg, 1968), and in various Orwell anthologies.

Riffaterre, Michael. 1959. Criteria for style analysis. Word 15. 154-174.

————. 1960. Stylistic context. Word 16.207-218.

Ryan, A. P. 1953. Wooster's progress. The New Statesman and Nation NS.45.737-738 (June 20, 1953).

Sampson, George. 1941. The concise Cambridge history of English literature. Cambridge (England) and New York: Cambridge University Press.

Sapir, Edward. 1922. Language. New York.

Schane, Sanford A. 1971. The phoneme revisited. Language 47.503-521.

Stevenson, Lionel. 1959. The antecedents of P. G. Wodehouse. Arizona Quarterly 5.226-234.

Swinnerton, Frank. 1935. The Georgian scene: a literary panorama. New York: Farrar and Straus. ["Chapter Seventeen: Later Novelists" 461-481, with "P. G. Wodehouse" 466-471.]

Tidwell, James N. 1947. The literary representation of the phonology of Southern dialect. Ohio State University dissertation.

————. (ed.). 1956. A treasury of American folk-humor. New York: Crown Publishers.

Usborne, Richard. 1961. Wodehouse at work. London: Herbert Jenkins.

Voorhees, Richard J. 1962. The jolly old world of P. G. Wodehouse. South Atlantic Quarterly 61.213-222 (Spring, 1962).

————. 1966. P. G. Wodehouse. New York: Twayne Publishers.

Wind, Herbert Warren. 1972. The world of P. G. Wodehouse. New York and Washington, D. C.: Praeger Publishers.

Index

All references are arranged in strictly alphabetical order. Titles of books are italicised, and those of short stories are in quotation-marks. Where no author's name is given for a book or short story, it is to be understood that it is by P. G. Wodehouse. References to notes are indicated by the letter n following the page-number. Fictional names (of persons, places, or things) are preceded by an asterisk.